Condemned and Crucified

Condemned and Crucified

by
John MacArthur, Jr.

WORD OF GRACE COMMUNICATIONS
P.O. Box 4000
Panorama City, CA 91412

All Scripture quotations, unless noted otherwise, are from the *New Scofield Reference Bible,* King James Version. Copyright © 1967 by Oxford University Press, Inc. Reprinted by permission.

Library of Congress Cataloging in Publication Data

MacArthur, John F.
   Condemned and crucified.

   (John MacArthur's Bible studies)
   Includes index.
   1. Jesus Christ—Passion.   2. Jesus Christ—
Crucifixion.   3. Atonement—Biblical teaching.
4. Passion narratives (Gospels) —Criticism, interpre-
tation, etc.   I. Title.   II. Series: MacArthur,
John F.   Bible studies.
BT431.M26   1987   232.9'6   86-31147
ISBN 0-8024-5349-X

1 2 3 4 5 6 7 Printing/LC/Year 91 90 89 88 87

Printed in the United States of America

Contents

These Bible studies are taken from messages delivered by Pastor-Teacher John MacArthur, Jr., at Grace Community Church in Panorama City, California. These messages have been combined into a 6-tape album entitled *Condemned and Crucified*. You may purchase this series either in an attractive vinyl cassette album or as individual cassettes. To purchase these tapes, request the album *Condemned and Crucified*, or ask for the tapes by their individual GC numbers. Please consult the current price list; then, send your order, making your check payable to:

WORD OF GRACE COMMUNICATIONS
P.O. Box 4000
Panorama City, CA 91412

Or call the following number:
818-982-7000

1
What Shall I Do with Jesus?—Part 1

Outline

Introduction
A. The Key Question
B. The Transition
    1. The Jewish trial
       a) The decision
       b) The deliverance
    2. The Roman trial

Lesson
I. The Accusation of the Jewish Leaders (vv. 11-12*a*)
A. The Questioning of the King (v. 11)
    1. The picture of phoniness (John 18:28)
    2. The problem of Pilate (John 18:29)
       a) The rule of the Herods
       b) The rule of Pilate
    3. The proof of perfection (John 18:30)
    4. The privilege of punishment (John 18:31)
       a) Extended (v. 31*a*)
       b) Refused (v. 31*b*)
    5. The plan of prophecy (John 18:32)
    6. The priorities of the prisoner (John 18:33-37)
    7. The proclamation of Pilate (John 18:38)
B. The Response of the Accusers (v. 12*a*)
    1. Empty talk
    2. Envious hearts

Introduction

A. The Key Question

Matthew 27:22 poses an important and fateful question: "Pilate saith unto them, What shall I do then with Jesus, who is called Christ?" Pilate was faced with an almost unbearable dilemma, a dilemma that every human on earth faces. The answer determines one's eternal destiny.

Tragically, Pilate chose the wrong response. He asked the right question, but instead of going to the right source, he went to the wrong source and received the wrong answer. It is my prayer that you will answer that question with the right answer.

B. The Transition

In Matthew 27:1-2, we find the transition from the Jewish trial of Christ to the Roman trial.

1. The Jewish trial

   Christ was being tried because the Jewish leaders wanted Him dead. The third phase of the Jewish trial was
   coming to a close. Christ stood before Annas, Caiaphas,
   and the Sanhedrin during the middle of the night and
   was before them once more in the morning so they
   could ratify what they did illegally during the night.
   (According to Jewish law it was illegal to try a man at
   night.) They condemned Him to death for blasphemy
   because He said He was the Son of God. Christ, however, merely stated the truth.

   To get rid of Christ, the Jewish leaders needed to get the
   Romans involved. Under the present Roman occupation, the Jews did not have the right of execution. The
   right of the sword, *ius gladii*, belonged only to Rome.
   Matthew 27:1-2 describes the last phase of the Jewish trial, which ended with the delivery of Jesus to Pilate. That
   began the first of three phases in the Roman trial.

   a) The decision

      Verse 1 says, "When the morning was come, all the
      chief priests and elders of the people took counsel
      against Jesus to put Him to death." That probably oc-
      curred early in the morning, around 5:00 A.M., before
      the dawn had begun to give its light. This meeting
      lasted perhaps no more than ten minutes. The pur-
      pose of it was to try to legalize the illegal decision
      they had come to in the middle of the night, between
      1:00 and 3:00 A.M. Jesus had been kept prisoner for
      two hours, and the leaders wanted to properly ratify
      their illegal decision in the daylight and in the right
      place—the judgment hall.

   b) The deliverance

      Verse 2 says, "When they had bound him, they led
      him away, and delivered him to Pontius Pilate, the
      governor." The Jewish leaders wanted the execution
      to be legal, so they wanted Rome to do it.

You may wonder why they didn't execute Jesus the way they did Stephen (Acts 7:58). Their action against Stephen was illegal—it was mob violence. The religious leaders didn't want to act as a mob in Jesus' case because they were trying to maintain a form of legality. They also wanted to do it as fast as possible so that the crowds, already beginning to rise with the dawn of a new day, didn't get involved, since Jesus was so popular with them. The leaders wanted everything done right, and that's why they wanted Pilate to execute Jesus. Pilate's judgment hall was probably located in Fort Antonia, which was north of the Temple ground.

2. The Roman trial

The Roman trial begins in Matthew 27:11. (Verses 3-10 are a digression describing the suicide of Judas.) Verse 11 says, "Jesus stood before the governor." The Roman trial had three phases: Christ appeared first before Pilate, then before Herod, and then again before Pilate. That makes a total of six phases to the trial of Jesus Christ, including the three Jewish phases.

Throughout all the phases, Jesus Christ is shown to be without fault. The Jewish leaders could not come up with a legitimate accusation against Him. The Spirit of God proved without a shadow of a doubt that Jesus is indeed the spotless Lamb of God who is fit to die for the sins of the world. In his gospel, Matthew continually presents the perfection, majesty, and purity of Christ. He does so especially well in his descriptions of the two trials. All the courts of men, combined with the efforts of demons, could not produce one legitimate accusation against Christ. Neither Caiaphas, Annas, the Sanhedrin, the false witnesses, Judas, Herod, nor Pilate could bring a legitimate accusation against Him. The record stands that He was killed because He was hated and rejected. The evil in men's hearts killed Christ.

As we study Matthew 27:11-26, we will see Christ's innocence on display.

Lesson

I. THE ACCUSATION OF THE JEWISH LEADERS (vv. 11-12a)

The lack of a legitimate accusation speaks volumes about the perfection of Christ.

A. The Questioning of the King (v. 11)

"Jesus stood before the governor; and the governor asked him, saying, Art thou the King of the Jews? And Jesus said unto him, Thou sayest."

Matthew doesn't show us that Pilate asked Jesus this question in response to the accusation the Jewish leaders brought against Him. To see that accusation, we need to look at John 18.

1. The picture of phoniness (John 18:28)

In the dawn around 5:00 A.M., Jesus was led to Pilate's judgment hall. Verse 28 says, "Then led they Jesus from Caiaphas." (Caiaphas presided over the third phase of the Jewish trial. It was held in his house.) Verse 28 continues, "They themselves [the Jewish leaders] went not into the judgment hall, lest they should be defiled; but that they might eat the passover." The Jews thought that contact with a Gentile meant defilement, and that included entering his house. The Talmud states that the dwelling places of the heathen are unclean because of the heathen practice of burying abortions in their houses (*Oholoth* ch. 18). So to maintain cleanliness as they approached the Passover, the religious leaders wanted to avoid defilement from a Gentile house. What hypocrisy to be preoccupied with a tradition like that while attempting to execute the Son of the living God! The religious leaders maintained a fastidious commitment to their religion while seeking to kill the Source of their religion.

2. The problem of Pilate (John 18:29)

Because the Jews wouldn't enter the judgment hall, Pilate had to come out. Verse 29 says, "Pilate then went out unto them, and said, What accusation bring ye against this man?" He wanted an indictment. He needed to know what he was trying Jesus for. That was the first legal thing that happened in the trial of Christ. Pilate was a Roman governor. He had been placed in Palestine to uphold Roman justice and rule.

a) The rule of the Herods

Pilate was not the only ruler. Herod Antipas ruled in Galilee and Peraea to the north. Herod Philip ruled the northeast, a less populated area. And Herod Archelaus had ruled in Judea, Samaria, and Idumaea. They were three sons of Herod the Great, an Idumean, who was once king of all Palestine. He had killed off some of his sons, but the remaining ones inherited parts of his kingdom. They were small-time kings, accompanied by much pomp and circumstance but not much power.

b) The rule of Pilate

The judicial processes and military might in Palestine resided in the hands of the Roman governor, who had been placed there to maintain the Roman peace—the *pax Romana*. Pilate had been governor since A.D. 26, and he would serve about ten years.

Since the Romans held the exclusive right of execution, the Jewish leaders had to approach Pilate. From the standpoint of Scripture, Jesus had to be executed by the Romans because it had been prophesied that He would die a Roman death. So Pilate held court outside the judgment hall. Jesus was inside, but the leaders remained outside.

3. The proof of perfection (John 18:30)

Verse 30 says, "They answered, and said unto him, If he were not a malefactor, we would not have delivered him up unto thee." They were saying, "What right have you to question our motives and our integrity? We wouldn't have brought Him to you if He weren't a criminal." Pilate asked a proper judicial question, but they couldn't give an answer. The Jewish leaders weren't looking for a judge; they were looking for an executioner. They didn't want another trial; they wanted Pilate to agree to take His life. The absence of any accusation here is another affirmation of Christ's perfection. Pilate didn't see Jesus as a threat. He knew of no crime He had committed. When he did ask for an accusation, the leaders had none to give.

4. The privilege of punishment (John 18:31)

   a) Extended (v. 31*a*)

   In verse 31 Pilate says to them, "Take ye him, and judge him according to your law." Pilate may have been giving them the right to execute Him. He simply didn't want to get involved. Pilate knew about Jesus. There's little doubt that when the Roman soldiers accompanied the Jewish leaders to take Jesus captive in the Garden of Gethsemane that they were there at Pilate's command. He knew what was going on, and he held an opinion about it.

   b) Refused (v. 31*b*)

   Verse 31 says, "The Jews, therefore, said unto him, It is not lawful for us to put any man to death." Nevertheless, they did it when they wanted to! They put Stephen to death. Later, they tried to kill Paul, but the Romans rescued him, moved him to Caesarea, and put him in a cell for two years to protect him. If the leaders wanted to kill Jesus badly enough, they would have. But they wanted to maintain an appearance of legality before the people.

5. The plan of prophecy (John 18:32)

   The plan of God demanded that Jesus be executed by the Romans. Verse 32 says, "That the saying of Jesus might be fulfilled, which he spoke, signifying what death he should die." Jesus had said He would be lifted up: "This he said, signifying what death he should die" (John 12:32-33). The Jewish leaders were fulfilling prophecy while thinking they were maintaining legality.

Refuting the Accusations

John 18:33 says, "Then Pilate entered into the judgment hall again, and called Jesus, and said unto him, Art thou the King of the Jews?" (cf. Matt. 27:11). Where did he get that accusation if the Jewish leaders didn't give it to him?

1. The accusations revealed

   Luke 23:2 says that the Jewish leaders concocted an accusation: "We found this fellow perverting the nation, and forbidding to give tribute to Caesar, saying that he himself is Christ, a king." They did not convict Him of that in their trial; they convicted Him of blasphemy because He claimed to be the Son of God. But they realized a charge of blasphemy wouldn't hold up in a Roman court, because the Romans wouldn't execute someone for his religious persuasion. So the Jews had to come up with an accusation that would appear to be high treason against Rome. The Romans had small toleration for rebels and revolutionaries. They had crucified many Jews who had tried to revolt against their government. The religious leaders also accused Christ of forbidding to pay taxes due Caesar and of telling others to do so as well. Then they accused Him of claiming to be a king—setting Himself up as a rival to Caesar.

2. The accusations refuted

   The leaders concocted those accusations on the spot, and of course they were false. Jesus didn't lead the nation of Israel into rebellion against Rome. He never led a social revolution. He never rebelled against Roman oppression—He submitted to the government. Jesus taught that if an official asked a man to carry his burden a mile, he should carry it two miles (Matt. 5:41). He taught people to respond properly to those in authority. He also taught people to pay their taxes. When Peter was asked if Jesus paid taxes, he said yes. Jesus affirmed that although they were technically exempt by being God's children, His followers were

14

to pay their taxes to avoid offending anyone (Matt. 17:24-27). He even said, "Render . . . unto Caesar the things which are Caesar's; and unto God, the things that are God's" (Matt. 22:21). A man should pay his taxes to the government but save his worship for the Lord. Jesus was a king but was not a threat to Caesar. When the people tried to make Him a king, He disappeared from their midst to avoid a revolution (John 6:15).

All the accusations were lies. They stand as a marvelous testimony to the perfection of Jesus Christ. He is the sinless, blameless Lamb of God, who came to take away the sins of the world.

6. The priorities of the prisoner (John 18:33-37)

When Pilate asked Jesus if He was the king of the Jews, Jesus answered, "Sayest thou this of thyself, or did others tell it thee of me?" (John 18:34). Pilate said, "Am I a Jew? Thine own nation and the chief priests have delivered thee unto me. What hast thou done?" (v. 35). Then Jesus answered Pilate, "My kingdom is not of this world; if my kingdom were of this world, then would my servants fight. . . . Thou sayest that I am a king. To this end was I born, and for this cause came I into the world" (vv. 36-37). Jesus was telling Pilate that His kingdom is a spiritual kingdom.

7. The proclamation of Pilate (John 18:38)

John 18:38 says that Pilate "went out again unto the Jews, and saith unto them, I find in him no fault at all." That was Pilate's verdict. The phrase "I find" has been carried down to courtroom proceedings of our day. When Pilate said he found no fault in Jesus, he was rendering a verdict of "not guilty." He knew Jesus was not guilty of being an insurrectionist who called people to avoid paying their taxes and to defy the government of Rome. No proof had been presented. Pilate knew he had no case against Jesus because Rome wasn't accusing Him of anything—it was strictly a Jewish problem.

Matthew 27:11 is a condensed version of John 18:28-38: "Jesus stood before the governor; and the governor asked him, saying, Art thou the King of the Jews? And Jesus said unto him, Thou sayest." After Jesus explained His kingdom to Pilate, the governor told the religious leaders that he found no fault in Him.

B. The Response of the Accusers (v. 12*a*)

"And when he was accused by the chief priests and elders."

Luke 23:5 says, "They were the more fierce, saying, He stirreth up the people, teaching throughout all Judaea, beginning from Galilee to this place." They put the heat on Pilate, who was no match for the furious hatred that was in the hearts of the leaders.

1. Empty talk

The accusation was empty talk; Pilate knew that. He had already stated that there was no fault in Christ. The religious court that mocked Jesus and the pagan court conducted by a coward named Pilate came up with the same verdict: not guilty. The Jewish leaders had to manufacture lies to kill Jesus Christ. Pilate could see through their plan. Was he to believe that the Jewish leaders, who despised the Roman presence, would ask that he execute someone because He was a threat to Rome? The thought was ridiculous. They would have joined hands with anyone who was a real threat to Rome; they certainly wouldn't have exposed him.

2. Envious hearts

Pilate knew that the Jews were motivated by envy (Matt. 27:18). They hated Christ because He could do what they couldn't. He could heal people, teach wisdom, and raise the dead. He was popular, and they weren't. Even a pagan unbeliever could see that the real issue was envy. Jesus never posed a threat to Rome. I'm sure Pilate suspected their motives when they asked him for a contingent of Roman soldiers to accompany them the night before.

There was no fault in Jesus. When Pilate told that to the crowd, he should have dismissed them. He should have moved in his soldiers and given Jesus the protection He needed. He should have done what justice required. Instead, he allowed the leaders to scream more accusations.

II. THE ATTITUDE OF THE LORD (vv. 12b-14)

The Lord's attitude in the midst of the accusations is another demonstration of His absolute perfection.

A. The Absolute Silence of Christ (v. 12b)

"He answered nothing."

While He was being fiercely accused, He answered nothing. When Pilate confronted Him another time, verse 14 says, "He answered him never a word." He said what He needed to say when He was on trial. The judge had rendered the verdict. There was nothing more to say. He knew He needed to die. That was the Father's will, and He was committed to it.

B. The Attempted Solution of Pilate (vv. 13-14)

"Then said Pilate unto him, Hearest thou not how many [great] things they witness against thee? And He answered him never a word, insomuch that the governor marveled greatly."

Pilate was amazed. He had seen a lot of prisoners and condemned many to death, but here was someone who was being accused of serious crimes, yet said nothing in His own defense. Pilate had seen a parade of criminals who would plead their innocence and cry for mercy. But Jesus remained quiet. Where was the troublesome revolutionary who was a threat to Rome? Where was the tax-dodging protester who was leading the nation in an insurrection? Where was the king who was a rival to Caesar? The only individual Pilate could see was a calm, peaceful man who, without any obvious reason, was offering Himself for execution. Pilate knew Jesus was innocent, and Jesus confirmed that by His silence. He was resolute—"a sheep before her shearers is dumb, so he openeth not his mouth" (Isa. 53:7). He willingly went to the cross.

Pilate's Dangerous Position

What was Pilate to do? He knew Jesus didn't deserve to die, yet he didn't want to disturb the crowd and create an incident. His life and career were on the line, and he knew it. When Pilate originally came to power, he made some big mistakes.

1. Mistake #1

   When Pilate was first appointed governor, he rode into Jerusalem with a large entourage of soldiers as a show of power. On the top of the banners that the soldiers carried were metal eagles. On top of each eagle was a molded image of Caesar. Prior governors had the sense to remove those kinds of things because the Jews believed them to be idols. The Jews didn't tolerate idols, so they rioted and demanded that he remove them from the banners. Pilate refused.

   After accomplishing what he wanted in Jerusalem, Pilate returned to the seacoast at Caesarea, the headquarters of his operation. Jews followed him for five days demanding that he remove the graven images. He refused, and the Jews persisted. Pilate finally called a meeting with the rioting Jews in the amphitheater in Caesarea, surrounded them with his soldiers, and told them that if they didn't stop their demands, he would cut off their heads. The Jews bared their necks, daring his soldiers to do so. They called his bluff.

   There was no way Pilate could go through with his ultimatum. He couldn't report to Rome that he had massacred many defenseless Jews. Furthermore, it could have led to a national revolution. Since he was sent to keep the peace, Pilate was forced to remove all the images. The Jews were now one up on him.

2. Mistake #2

   Later in his reign, Pilate realized there was a need for a better water supply in Jerusalem, so he decided to build an aqueduct to bring in more water. To do so, he took money out of the Temple treasury—money that was devoted to God. That fomented another riot. Pilate dealt with it by sending soldiers into a huge crowd. At a given signal, they clubbed and stabbed many people to death.

3. Mistake #3

Pilate established residence in the city of Jerusalem and had shields made for his soldiers. On the shields he had engraved the likeness of Tiberius, the emperor. To the Jewish people, that was an emblem of a false god, so they demanded that the shields be changed. Pilate refused. The Jews reported Pilate's actions to Tiberius, who sent word to Pilate to change the shields immediately.

Pilate couldn't afford another report to Tiberius. He couldn't afford another riot or any kind of revolution. He was truly in a difficult place. He had enough of a sense of justice to know what was right, but he was a coward because he feared what would happen if he released Christ. Whatever would happen would most likely cost him his job. It might have even cost him his life, because it was not unlike Tiberius to execute ineffective governors.

1. Deferring to Herod's Authority

When Pilate heard the religious leaders say that Jesus first started to stir up the people in Galilee (Luke 23:5), he realized there was a potential solution to his problem. Luke 23:7 says, "As soon as he knew that he [Jesus] belonged unto Herod's jurisdiction, he sent him to Herod, who himself also was at Jerusalem at that time." The time was still around 5:00 A.M. Herod Antipas was the ruler of Galilee, yet he functioned under the yoke of Rome. Pilate hoped he could eliminate his problem by passing off Christ to Herod.

a) The curiosity of Herod

Herod Antipas knew about Jesus because of His great ministry in Galilee. After all, Jesus had virtually removed disease from Galilee. Christ judiciously avoided the city of Tiberius during His Galilean ministry simply because Herod's headquarters were there. Herod Antipas had John the Baptist beheaded. He was an immoral, murderous man.

Jesus avoided Herod, but Herod was curious about Jesus. When Herod heard he was finally going to have the opportunity to meet Him, he was happy (Luke 23:8). He wanted to see Jesus perform a miracle.

b) The countenance of Christ

Jesus was rushed off early in the morning as Herod set up a court of his own. Luke 23:9 says, "Then he [Herod] questioned him in many words; but he answered him nothing." Jesus owed nothing to Herod because Herod did not have the right to judge a man in Palestine; Pilate held that right, and he had already pronounced his verdict. But why didn't Jesus tell Herod about His kingdom, as He did for Pilate? Herod already knew about Christ's kingdom; he had heard the preaching of John the Baptist. He heard everything there was to hear about the teaching of Jesus.

c) The contempt of Herod's men

The chief priests were also present at this particular hearing before Herod. Luke 23:10 says, "The chief priests and scribes stood and vehemently accused him [Christ]." Herod perceived the whole affair as a joke. He didn't see Jesus as a rival king or an insurrectionist. Christ stood before Herod with a face that had been beaten black and blue from blows delivered by the Temple guard in the hearing before Caiaphas (Matt. 26:67-68). He hardly looked like a threat to Roman security or Herod's throne. Luke 23:11 says, "Herod, with his men of war, treated him with contempt, and mocked him, and arrayed him in a gorgeous robe [a bright, white robe that was commonly worn by Jewish kings]." Nevertheless, Herod came up with no accusation.

2. Declaring Herod's affirmation

In reporting the results of Herod's interrogation to the crowd, Pilate said, "Ye have brought this man unto me, as one that perverteth the people; and, behold, I, having

20

examined him before you, have found no fault in this man touching those things of which ye accuse him; no, nor yet Herod; for I sent you to him, and, lo, nothing worthy of death is done by him" (Luke 23:14-15). So Pilate affirmed that Herod's verdict was the same as his. Jesus hadn't done anything. He was no insurrectionist or threat to security.

The accusation of the Jews demonstrated the perfection of Christ. The attitude of Christ before Pilate and Herod also demonstrated His perfection. Jesus answered nothing because there was no crime. So even the wrath of men vindicates Christ.

III. THE ANIMOSITY OF THE CROWD (vv. 15-18, 20-23, 25)

A. The Concession of Pilate (vv. 15-18)

The first and second phase of the Roman trial ended with an acquittal: both Pilate and Herod found no fault in Jesus. Now Christ was back in Pilate's hands, initiating a third phase to the trial. Pilate could have ended the trial after the first or second phase. But he was trapped. He couldn't defy the Jews without starting a riot, which could be fatal to his career—and possibly his life. So what could he do? He had another plan.

1. The customary observance (v. 15)

"Now at that feast [Passover] the governor was accustomed to releasing unto the people a prisoner, whom they would [desired]."

As a concession to a conquered people, the governor would release a criminal during the Passover (Luke 23:18; Mark 15:8).

2. The criminal Barabbas (v. 16)

"They had then a notable prisoner, called Barabbas."

Barabbas was not just another common criminal; he was well known. We don't know anything about his background. Some think his name means "son of the father"; some think it is "son of the rabbi." According to John 18:40, he was a robber. Mark 15:7 and Luke 23:19 say he was an insurrectionist and a murderer. He must have been a threat to the Jews as well as the Romans. He was an arch-criminal who was a severe threat to the safety of the population. He was due to be crucified. I believe Jesus died on the cross that was meant for Barabbas, as He was crucified between two of his thieving partners (Mark 15:7).

3. The calculating Pilate (v. 17)

"Therefore, when they were gathered together, Pilate said unto them, Whom will ye that I release unto you? Barabbas, or Jesus, who is called Christ?"

Pilate added the phrase "who is called Christ" twice after the name Jesus—once in verse 17 and once in verse 22—to emphasize the difference between Jesus and Barabbas. So Pilate stated that Jesus was called the Anointed, another way of saying king.

What did Pilate have in mind? He knew whom the leaders would choose. But Pilate wanted to pit the leaders against the people. He knew about the popularity of Jesus, how the population treated Him in His triumphal entry. It was approaching 6:00 A.M. (cf. John 19:14), and the people were beginning to gather. Pilate knew the leaders would want Jesus crucified but was sure the people would want Jesus released. Even a pagan like Pilate knew the difference between Christ and a criminal. Thus we have another wonderful testimony to the innocence of Jesus Christ.

4. The covetous leaders (v. 18)

"For he knew that for envy they [the Jewish leaders] had delivered him."

Pilate believed that the people wouldn't be motivated by envy. They were the recipients of Jesus' ministry; they weren't in competition with Him as the leaders were.

B. The Campaign of the Leaders (v. 20)

"The chief priests and elders persuaded the multitude that they should ask for Barabbas, and destroy Jesus."

I believe God allowed for an interruption from Pilate's wife (v. 19), which gave the Jewish leaders time to stir up the crowd against Jesus. Remember, it was the plan of God that Jesus die. Pilate's plan might have worked, but the people were convinced by the leaders because they were fickle. Four days had passed since Jesus came into town, and He had not performed any miracles or overthrown the Romans. Since both Pilate and Herod had found no fault in Him, the crowd might have concluded that anyone whom Pilate said was not a threat was certainly no Messiah. They believed the Messiah would come to overthrow Rome, but here Rome was saying Jesus was blameless. Could anyone Pilate approved of be their Messiah? The leaders used whatever leverage they could gain as they moved through the crowd. Mark 15:11 says, "The chief priests stirred up the people, that he should rather release Barabbas unto them." They wanted to destroy Jesus. By the time Pilate's attention was turned back to the people, he had a worse problem because the crowd and the leaders had become one.

C. The Choice of the Crowd (vv. 21-23)

1. Release Barabbas (v. 21)

"The governor answered and said unto them, Which of the two will ye that I release unto you? They said, Barabbas."

I'm sure Pilate was jolted. He had underestimated the power of the leaders and overestimated the heart of the people. He had no concept of the demons of hell that were involved in the scene, nor did he know anything about the plan of God.

2. Crucify Christ (vv. 22-23)

"Pilate saith unto them, What shall I do then with Jesus, who is called Christ? They all say unto him, Let him be crucified. And the governor said, Why, what evil hath he done? But they cried out the more, saying, Let him be crucified."

They wanted Jesus' blood, and nothing Pilate did would change that. If he wouldn't uphold simple justice, why should he expect a mob to do so? Pilate was in a panic. He didn't want to violate justice, but he also didn't want to start a riot.

When he asked, "Why, what evil hath he done?" (v. 23), we see that when every aspect of the trial of Christ was finished, He remained blameless. The people cried louder and more vehemently for Jesus to be crucified. The whole crowd was out of control, and Pilate couldn't handle it.

D. The Curse of the Blood (v. 25)

"Then answered all the people, and said, His blood be on us, and on our children."

The Jewish crowd said they would be responsible for His blood. In their mindless rage they damned themselves. That was the verdict of the nation Israel on their Messiah. No wonder Romans 11:20 says they have been broken off the stalk of blessing and have known the chastening of God. Nevertheless forgiveness is available for the Jewish person just as it is for any individual who comes to Christ. In fact, the gospel is to be preached to the Jew first and also to the Gentile (Rom. 1:16).

The nation soon forgot that they took responsibility for Jesus' death. After the apostle Peter began to preach in Jerusalem, the Jewish leaders said, "Ye have filled Jerusalem with your doctrine, and intend to bring this man's blood upon us" (Acts 5:28). The apostles didn't do it; the nation brought it on themselves. They affirmed their own guilt in the death of Jesus Christ. That is yet another testimony to the innocence of Christ.

1. The field of blood

   The field that the Jewish leaders purchased with the money used to betray Christ was called "The Field of Blood." Everyone knew it was blood money paid to a traitor for betraying an innocent man. The place where Judas fell after hanging himself was called the same thing. Everything about Jesus was pure, while around Him hovered evil, dishonest, murderous people.

2. The forgiveness of Christ

   As Christ was being crucified, He said, "Father, forgive them; for they know not what they do" (Luke 23:34). Ever since, forgiveness has been available for both Jew and Gentile.

   The Jewish people took on themselves the blood guiltiness for Christ's death. In so doing, they gave testimony to the whole world that it was their responsibility.

Focusing on the Facts

1. What is one question every person must answer at some time (see p. 8)?
2. What did the Jewish leaders need to do to have Christ executed (see p. 9)?
3. Why didn't the Jews want to execute Jesus as they later did Stephen (see p. 10)?
4. How did Matthew present Christ throughout his gospel (see p. 10)?
5. Why were Jesus' accusers unwilling to enter the judgment hall of the governor (John 18:28; see p. 11)?
6. Who were the rulers in Palestine? How much power did each one hold (see p. 12)?
7. Why did the Jewish leaders criticize Pilate for asking them for an accusation (see pp. 12-13)?
8. Whose plan was it that Jesus be executed at the hands of the Romans (see p. 13)?
9. What accusations did the Jewish leaders bring against Jesus before Pilate (Luke 23:2; see p. 14)?
10. Explain why those accusations were false (see pp. 14-15).

11. What verdict did Pilate give based on the accusations he heard (John 18:38; see p. 15)?
12. What motivated the Jews to have Jesus killed (Matt. 27:18; see p. 16)?
13. Why did Jesus give no answer when the religious leaders accused Him (see p. 17)?
14. Why was Pilate amazed at Jesus' silence (see p. 17)?
15. Describe the three events that put Pilate in the dangerous position of having to decide what to do with Jesus (see pp. 18-19).
16. Why did Pilate send Jesus to Herod (Luke 23:7; see p. 19)?
17. Why did Christ not need to respond to any of Herod's questions (see p. 20)?
18. What did Herod's men do to Jesus after He had been questioned by Herod (Luke 23:11; see p. 20)?
19. Why was it customary for the governor to release a prisoner at Passover (see p. 21)?
20. Who was Barabbas (see pp. 21-22)?
21. What did Pilate want to happen when he offered the people a choice between Jesus and Barabbas (see p. 22)?
22. How were the chief priests and elders able to foil Pilate's plan (Matt. 27:19-20; see p. 23)?
23. How did the Jewish people affirm their guilt in the death of Jesus Christ (Matt. 27:25; see p. 24)?

Pondering the Principles

1. In his gospel, Matthew presents the perfection of Jesus Christ. Over the course of the next week, read the gospel of Matthew. You may want to read four chapters a day. As you read, record each instance where Matthew presents Christ as perfect. When you finish, review your list. Then praise God for Christ and His plan of redemption.

2. Throughout the three phases of the Roman trial of Christ, Jesus stands blameless. No accusations that could be proved were ever brought against Him. The reason is simple: Jesus Christ is sinless. Look up the following verses about the sinlessness of Christ: Isaiah 53:9; 2 Corinthians 5:21; Hebrews 4:15; 1 Peter 1:19; 2:22; and 1 John 3:5. How might you apply those verses to your own life? Thank God for supplying such a perfect Savior to die in your place.

2
What Shall I Do with Jesus?—Part 2

Outline

Introduction
A. The Person of Christ
 1. Jesus is God
 2. Jesus is the perfect God-man
 3. Jesus is the promised Savior
B. The Perfection of Christ
 1. He is holy
 2. He is loving

Review
 I. The Accusation of the Jewish Leaders (vv. 11-12*a*)
 II. The Attitude of the Lord (vv. 12*b*-14)
III. The Animosity of the Crowd (vv. 15-18, 20-23, 25)
    A. The Concession of Pilate (vv. 15-18)
    B. The Campaign of the Leaders (v. 20)
    C. The Choice of the Crowd (vv. 21-23)
    D. The Curse of the Blood (v. 25)

Lesson
IV. The Apprehension of the Wife (v. 19)
    A. The Setting (v. 19*a*)
    B. The Message (v. 19*b-c*)
      1. Her conviction of Christ's righteousness (v. 19*b*)
        a) The warning
        b) The consequence
      2. Her suffering in a dream (v. 19*c*)

V. The Acquiescence of the Governor (vv. 24, 26)
   A. Pilate's Intimidation Continued (v. 24a)
   B. Pilate's Innocence Claimed (v. 24b-c)
     1. The tradition of the Old Testament (v. 24b)
     2. The testimony of Pilate (v. 24c)
   C. Pilate's Intention Circumvented (v. 26)
     1. The suffering of Christ
       a) The scourging
       b) The satire
     2. The sarcasm of Pilate
       a) His cowardice
       b) His cruelty
       c) His challenge
     3. The scorn of the Jews
     4. The shame of Pilate
       a) His ultimate fear
       b) His ultimate fate
          (1) The source of Pilate's judgment
            (a) The suspicion of Pilate
            (b) The silence of Christ
          (2) The source of Pilate's authority
       c) His ultimate failure
     5. The sentencing of the King

Conclusion

Introduction

Matthew 27:22 records that Pilate asked, "What shall I do then with Jesus, who is called Christ?" That is a question everyone must answer. I would like to pose another question: Why must every person answer that question? What is it about Jesus Christ that lays such a claim on every heart?

   A. The Person of Christ

     1. Jesus is God

       a) He is the possessor of God's names

          Matthew 1:23 says, "They shall call his name Immanuel, which, being interpreted, is God with us."

In Acts 3:14 the apostle Peter calls Jesus the "Holy One"—an Old Testament name distinctly given to God (e.g., Ps. 16:10; Isa. 48:17).

b) He is one with God the Father

John 8:19 says to know Christ is to know the Father. John 15:23 says to hate Him is to hate the Father. John 14:9 says to see Him is to see the Father. John 5:23 says to honor Him is to honor the Father. And Mark 9:37 and Matthew 10:40 say to receive Him is to receive the Father.

c) He is omnipresent

Jesus said, "Lo, I am with you always" (Matt. 28:20). Omnipresence is true only of God.

d) He is eternal

Hebrews 13:8 says, "Jesus Christ [is] the same yesterday, and today, and forever."

e) He is the Creator of the world

John 1:3 says, "All things were made by him; and without him was not anything made that was made."

f) He is able to forgive sin

Repeatedly in His ministry, Jesus said, "Thy sins are forgiven thee" (Mark 2:9). That is another divine prerogative.

g) He is to be worshiped as God

Philippians 2:10 says, "At the name of Jesus every knee should bow, of things in heaven, and things in earth, and things under the earth."

Scripture clearly indicates that Jesus Christ is fully God. Since He is God, everyone is obligated to respond to Him.

2. Jesus is the perfect God-man

   Just because Jesus is God doesn't mean He is any less man. How do we know? He was born. He was circumcised. He grew. He had a human name. He had flesh and blood. He was hungry. He wept. He thirsted. He slept. He was weary. He suffered. He was tempted. He was wounded. He died. And He was buried. All are indications of His humanness. No one like Jesus has ever existed. He has the right to make tremendous demands on our lives because of who He is.

3. Jesus is the promised Savior

   Jesus came into the world not only to show us what God is like, but also to bring us to God. The prophets outlined the details of His life with astounding accuracy.

   a) His birth

      Micah 5:2 says it would occur in Bethlehem. Daniel 9:24-27 gives the approximate date. Isaiah 7:14 tells us it would be a virgin birth. Genesis 9:26 indicates He would come from the Semitic line. Genesis 22:18 says He would come from the line of Abraham. Genesis 49:10 says He would come from the tribe of Judah. Second Samuel 7:13 says He would come through the seed of David.

   b) His life

      Hosea 11:1 indicates He would be taken to Egypt. Deuteronomy 18:15 says He would be a prophet like Moses. Psalm 22:10 indicates He would trust God from His birth onward. Isaiah 9:1-2 says He would begin His ministry in Galilee. Isaiah 11:2 says He would be anointed by God's Spirit. Isaiah 53:4 says He would carry our griefs and sorrows. Zechariah 9:9 says He would enter Jerusalem on a colt. Isaiah 35:5-6 indicates He would perform miracles.

c) His death

Psalm 2:1-3 indicates that kings would plot His death (cf. Acts 4:25-28). Psalm 22:1 says He would die forsaken by God. Psalm 22:6-8 says He would be scorned and mocked. Zechariah 11:12 says He would be betrayed for thirty pieces of silver. Zechariah 12:10 says He would be smitten and pierced by His own people. Isaiah 52:14 says He would be brutally treated. Isaiah 53:5, 10 says He would die for the world's iniquity. Psalm 22:18 says His garments would be divided. Psalm 41:9 says He would be betrayed by a friend. Psalm 34:20 indicates that none of His bones would be broken. Isaiah 50:6 says His beard would be plucked out and that He would be spit on.

d) His resurrection

Psalm 16:10 says He would never see corruption. Psalm 22:21 indicates He would conquer death.

e) His present work

Psalm 110:4 indicates He would function as a priest. Amos 9:11 says He would sit on David's throne.

B. The Perfection of Christ

1. He is holy

His holiness demonstrates His perfection. Jesus was free from defilement. He loved righteousness, hated sin, was victorious over temptation, rebuked sinners, and will judge unbelievers.

2. He is loving

Jesus' love knows no limits. He loves the Father, and He loves lost, ungodly sinners. He loves His own—the church. He loves children. Jesus demonstrated His love by becoming poor, giving His life, forgiving sin, seeking the lost, healing the sick, supplying the needs of others, and strengthening His people. He showed compassion on those who were lost, hungry, sick, blind, demonized, grieved, repentant—and even dead!

Jesus was also prayerful, meek, humble, righteous, good, faithful, truthful, just, and self-denying. In every way He is the spotless, perfect Lamb of God who came to die for the sins of the world.

It is this Jesus of whom Pilate asks: "What then shall I do with Jesus who is called the Christ?" Jesus Christ came into the world to redeem the world from sin, to bring salvation, to remove transgressions, to destroy Satan, and to set up an eternal kingdom of peace and glory for those who love and believe in Him. To do so it was essential that He die for sin. He paid the penalty as our substitute and rose again that we might live forever. The destiny of every human being hinges on what he does with Jesus Christ.

Review

Jesus' earthly ministry came to a climax as He entered into Jerusalem for His final Passover. A few days later Judas betrayed Him into the hands of the Jewish leaders. There were three phases in the Jewish trial followed by three phases in the Roman trial. It is the Roman trial we are looking at in Matthew 27:11-26.

I. THE ACCUSATION OF THE JEWISH LEADERS (vv. 11-12a; see pp. 11-17)

II. THE ATTITUDE OF THE LORD (vv. 12b-14; see pp. 17-21)

III. THE ANIMOSITY OF THE CROWD (vv. 15-18, 20-23, 25; see pp. 21-25)

A. The Concession of Pilate (vv. 15-18; see pp. 21-23)

B. The Campaign of the Leaders (v. 20; see p. 23)

C. The Choice of the Crowd (vv. 21-23; see pp. 23-24)

Pilate asked what he should do with Christ after he discovered that the people wanted him to release Barabbas and not Christ (Matt. 27:22). Luke 23:20-22 adds some insight into this scene: "Pilate, therefore, willing to release Jesus, spoke again to them. But they cried, saying, Crucify him! Crucify him! And he said unto them the third time, Why, what evil hath he done? I have found no cause of death in him. I will, therefore, chastise him, and let him go." Since Pilate found no fault in Him, why was he going to chastise Him? It was an act of condescension on Pilate's part. He wanted to appease the bloodthirsty cries of the people. But that wasn't going to be enough. Verses 23-24 say, "They were urgent with loud voices, requiring that he might be crucified. And the voices of them and of the chief priests prevailed. And Pilate gave sentence that it should be as they required." Incredible. On five separate occasions Pilate and Herod combined to announce the innocence of Jesus Christ. Then Pilate sentenced Him to death. Verse 25 says, "He released unto them him that, for sedition and murder, was cast into prison, whom they had desired; but he delivered Jesus to their will."

D. The Curse of the Blood (v. 25; see pp. 24-25)

Lesson

IV. THE APPREHENSION OF THE WIFE (v. 19)

Matthew 27:19 shows what interrupted Pilate and allowed the leaders to stir up the crowd.

A. The Setting (v. 19a)

"When he [Pilate] was seated on the judgment seat."

Pilate was presiding over the trial of Jesus at the official seat of authority. Since the Jewish leaders wouldn't go into the judgment hall, Pilate came out on the porch. As he took his seat outside, that constituted a genuine judicial act because he was seated on the judgment seat.

B. The Message (v. 19*b-c*)

    1. Her conviction of Christ's righteousness (v. 19*b*)

"His wife sent unto him, saying, Have thou nothing to do with that righteous man."

    a) The warning

Pilate must have had high regard for his wife's opinion because he stopped the proceedings to hear what she had to say. What was her verdict on Jesus Christ? That He was righteous. No doubt they had discussed Jesus the night before when Pilate gave permission for his soldiers to accompany the Jews when they went to capture Jesus. Pilate certainly was not oblivious to what was going on in the land of Palestine. He knew Jesus had virtually banished disease from the land. He knew what had happened in the past week. He heard about Jesus' cleansing of the Temple. He knew Jesus had been hailed as Messiah when He first entered the city. I'm sure that even word of Lazarus's resurrection had reached him. Pilate knew envy motivated the Jewish leaders to want Jesus dead (v. 18).

Pilate's wife was convinced that Jesus was a righteous man—and that is the testimony of a pagan. The nation of Israel, with all they knew from the prophets, promises, and law of God, cursed their Messiah, took His blood on themselves, and killed Him. Yet a pagan who knew nothing testified that Jesus was righteous. What a condemnation of the people of Israel! Their actions betrayed a denial of their own Scriptures.

    b) The consequence

Pilate's wife didn't want her husband to get involved with Jesus because He was righteous. She was fearful of the consequences. She was right, because later on Pilate was removed from Palestine and sent to Gaul. He there committed suicide according to tradition. Why did he commit suicide? For the same reason Judas did. Neither could deal with the tremendous guilt of having betrayed the only perfectly righteous person who ever lived. According to psychologists, the primary cause of suicide is retribution: it is a self-inflicted punishment. The ultimate crime brought ultimate punishment.

2. Her suffering in a dream (v. 19c)

"I have suffered many things this day in a dream because of him."

Her dream may have been a providential act of God. I believe God was involved because only He could send the messenger at the right moment to allow time for the Jewish leaders to stir up the crowd. Jesus had to die. Everything that happened in this trial was by the predetermined plan of God (Acts 2:23). What Pilate's wife knew about Jesus certainly could have been directed by the Spirit of God into a dream that filled her heart with fear. She suffered because of it. We don't know what she thought might happen to her husband in dealing with Jesus, but her worst fears were coming true because he was trapped into making an unjust decision about Jesus.

V. THE ACQUIESCENCE OF THE GOVERNOR (vv. 24, 26)

A. Pilate's Intimidation Continued (v. 24a)

"When Pilate saw that he could prevail [gain] nothing, but that rather a tumult [Gk., thorubos, "riot"] was made."

Pilate couldn't afford another riot. The last one brought about a direct rebuke from Tiberius Caesar. He certainly recalled the previous occasions when riots occurred because of his obstinate refusal to bend to the wishes of the Jews (see pp. 18-19). Here was a similar situation.

One thing we can say about Pilate is that he tried to get Jesus off his hands. He sent Him to Herod. He suggested that He be released at the Passover. He and Herod rendered five verdicts of His innocence. He appealed to the people. He tried to give Him back to the Jews so that they would try Him themselves (v. 24c). However, they refused because they wanted Jesus' execution to appear legal. Nothing Pilate tried worked because Jesus had to be crucified to fulfill Scripture.

B. Pilate's Innocence Claimed (v. 24b-c)

1. The tradition of the Old Testament (v. 24b)

"He took water, and washed his hands before the multitude."

Pilate's actions followed a Jewish tradition based on Deuteronomy 21:6-9. When someone was murdered in ancient times in the cities of Israel, the elders of the city were responsible to find the guilty party. Sometimes that was not possible. So the elders would come to a public place in the city and wash their hands in front of the people. That signified that since they tried their best, yet were unable to find the murderer, they were free from the guilt of the murder.

God does not tolerate unrequited blood. That is a basic principle in Scripture and is why capital punishment is instituted in Genesis 9:6. When Cain killed Abel, God said that Abel's blood cried to Him from the ground.

2. The testimony of Pilate (v. 24c)

"I am innocent of the blood of this righteous person. See ye to it."

The people followed that statement by screaming, "His blood be on us" (v. 25). The Jewish nation took the guilt for the blood of Christ. When Pilate said, "See ye to it," he might have been giving them the right to kill Jesus.

Pilate tried to get rid of Jesus, but he couldn't. Again he affirmed the innocence of Christ. Do you think Pilate wished Jesus were guilty? Of course—that would have solved all his problems. If he could have found one thing that made Jesus guilty, he could have executed Him with a clear conscience. Pilate was like Judas. Do you think Judas wanted to find one flaw in the life of

Christ that could justify his betrayal of Him? Yes. Do you think Annas and Caiaphas wanted to find one thing wrong with Jesus to justify their hatred of Him? Certainly. The same is true of the false witnesses. He was innocent, whereas everyone around Him was guilty!

C. Pilate's Intention Circumvented (v. 26)

"Then released he Barabbas unto them; and when he had scourged Jesus, he delivered him to be crucified."

It was Pilate's intention to scourge Jesus and then let Him go. However, things didn't work out that way. Matthew doesn't give us the details of what happened immediately after the scourging but John does, beginning with 19:1.

1. The suffering of Christ

   a) The scourging

   A Roman scourge had a short wooden handle that held a series of leather thongs threaded with bits of lead, brass, and bones sharpened to a razor's edge. The man was taken by the wrists and tied to a post, his body taut. Two men, one on each side, would whip him across the flanks and back, exposing arteries, veins, and entrails. That often brought about death. Scourging was often done before crucifixion to speed up the victim's death on the cross. It was torture beyond description.

   The Jews gave forty lashes, save one. We don't know how many the Romans administered. We do know that Jesus couldn't carry His own cross all the way to the place of execution because He was so weak. If there ever was a man of strength, it was Jesus, because a man without sin would be a man of strength. However, He had been beaten so badly that even He couldn't carry the cross.

   b) The satire

   John 19:2 says that after the scourging, "the soldiers platted a crown of thorns, and put it on his head."

They made a crown to mock Him and crushed it onto His brow. Then they put a purple robe on Him. In verse 3 they say, "Hail, King of the Jews!" The Greek text indicates that they continually hailed Him and struck Him.

The soldiers put kingly garb on Jesus because they were playing a game. If you were to visit the grounds of Fort Antonia in Jerusalem, you would find that the *gabbatha*—the pavement—is still there. On it you can see markings of games the Roman soldiers played. The soldiers picked on prisoners or mentally retarded children as a way to pass the time. They would dress them in certain ways and then mock them. That's what they did to Jesus. Matthew added that they spit on Him and smashed His head with a reed (Matt. 27:30).

2. The sarcasm of Pilate

   a) His cowardice

   After the game was through, Pilate went before the mob and said, "Behold, I bring him forth to you, that ye may know that I find no fault in him" (John 19:4). Why did he bring Jesus before the people after having Him scourged? Because He was trying to quench their thirst for blood. He was exposing a pathetic man—a man whose face had been beaten black and blue, whose head had been crushed, and whose back and sides had been ripped raw so that His internal organs were visible. It is this picture of Jesus that Isaiah 53:2 was referring to: "There is no beauty that we should desire him."

   b) His cruelty

   Then Pilate said, "Behold the man" (v. 5). He wanted Jesus to look so bad that the people would want to let Him go. He was hoping they would say, "We can't take anymore. This inhumane treatment is more than we can stand!" But the crowd had tasted blood—and they wanted more.

c) His challenge

> Verse 6 says, "When the chief priests, therefore, and the officers saw him, they cried out, saying, Crucify him, crucify him! Pilate saith unto them, Take ye him, and crucify him; for I find no fault in him." The leaders hounded Pilate to crucify Christ because they wouldn't kill Him themselves. However, Jesus couldn't have been killed by the Jews because He said He would be lifted up (John 12:32-33). If He had been killed by Jews, He would have been stoned.

3. The scorn of the Jews

> John 19:7 says, "The Jews answered him, We have a law, and by our law he ought to die, because he made himself the Son of God." Christ's so-called blasphemy (Mark 14:61-64) was what really bothered the Jewish leaders.

4. The shame of Pilate

a) His ultimate fear

> Pilate heard something he didn't want to hear when the Jews said Jesus claimed to be the Son of God. Verse 8 says, "When Pilate, therefore, heard that saying, he was the more afraid." Pilate knew Jesus could heal the sick and raise the dead. He knew He had unique and strange powers. Over the period of an hour Pilate had seen Christ display remarkable personal characteristics, especially the calmness with which He maintained His silence. However, Christ's claim to be the Son of God frightened him more than anything else. Pilate's pagan mind had been conditioned to the existence of many gods. Superstitious fear made him wonder if he was really dealing with the son of a god.

b) His ultimate fate

(1) The source of Pilate's judgment

(*a*) The suspicion of Pilate

Pilate brought Jesus back into the judgment hall and said to Him, "From where art thou?" (v. 9). Two of the three incidents that got Pilate into trouble with the Jews had to do with false gods. The first was the image of Caesar above the eagles on the standards that his soldiers carried. The second was the engraving of Caesar on the shields of the soldiers. Pilate didn't want to get involved with the Jews one more time over the issue of false gods.

Satan initiated a diabolical plan through the Jewish leaders, which forced Pilate into a problem similar to the ones he had faced before. He had already been reprimanded by Rome for interfering in the Jewish religion. So Pilate wanted to know if the Jewish leaders were trying to have the son of a false god put to death.

(*b*) The silence of Christ

John 19:9 says, "Jesus gave him no answer." He knew Pilate's heart. Pilate had already rejected the truth. Whether Jesus was the Son of God was not a matter for Rome to decide. Pilate and Herod had combined to render a verdict of innocent five times already, so there was nothing for Christ to say.

(2) The source of Pilate's authority

John 19:10-11 says, "Then saith Pilate unto him, Speakest thou not unto me? Knowest thou not that I have power to crucify thee, and have power to release thee? Jesus answered, Thou couldest have no power at all against me, except it were given thee from above; therefore, he that delivered me unto thee hath the greater sin." The people who delivered Christ to Pilate were the greater sinners. Pilate sinned through weakness—he was just a pawn in the game—but the Jewish leaders sinned through willful hatred. There are degrees to rejecting Christ, and the severer the rejection, the severer the punishment in hell.

c) His ultimate failure

Verse 12 says, "From then on Pilate sought to release him." Pilate wanted Jesus out of his hands because he was afraid of one more incident with the Jews involving a false god. Verse 12 continues, "But the Jews cried out, saying, If thou let this man go, thou art not Caesar's friend; whosoever maketh himself a king speaketh against Caesar." They brought up a political issue. They told Pilate he wouldn't be serving Caesar's best interests by showing complicity with an insurrectionist. Pilate knew if that report got back to Caesar, he was through.

5. The sentencing of the King

John 19:13-15 says, "When Pilate, therefore, heard that saying, he brought Jesus forth, and sat down in the judgment seat in a place that is called The Pavement, but in the Hebrew, Gabbatha. And it was the preparation of the passover, and about the sixth hour [6:00 A.M.]; and he saith unto the Jews, Behold, your King! But they cried out, Away with him, away with him, crucify him! Pilate saith unto them, Shall I crucify your king? The chief priests answered, We have no king but Caesar." It was one thing for the Jewish nation to claim responsibility for Christ's blood, but to say they had no king but Caesar was their final condemnation. Is it any wonder that God destroyed Jerusalem, the center of their religion? Is it any wonder that for centuries they have been under the judgment of God, except for the remnant who are called by His grace through faith in Christ? It's frightening! They rejected their true King and accepted an earthly king for the sake of convenience.

Conclusion

Jesus Christ is innocent, perfect, and holy. The Old Testament said that the lamb offered for sin must be without spot or blemish (Ex. 12:5). All that Christ endured through the mock trials proved He was suitable to serve as the perfect Lamb of God to die for the sins of the world. The world of religious and irreligious men, inspired by Satan himself, could not find one spot or blemish on this Lamb. Thus Jesus was the perfect sacrifice. Although His visage was marred by the physical abuse He suffered, He shines forth as the beautiful Lamb of God.

How could the Jewish leaders and Pilate agree to sentence Christ to death? Acts 2:23 says He was "delivered by the determinant counsel and foreknowledge of God." Isaiah 53:6 says, "The Lord hath laid on him the iniquity of us all." God called Jesus to be the Savior.

Jesus wasn't on trial, but everyone else was. You're on trial, too. What you do with Jesus Christ determines your eternal destiny. What are your options? You can hate Him as the Jewish leaders did. You can reject him as the fickle crowd did. You can mock Him as Herod did. You can have nothing to do with Him as Pilate's wife did. Or you can get rid of Him as Pilate did. Whatever you choose will be a choice for eternity. Why not reject all those choices and choose to follow in the steps of Christ and receive the blessings of God forever?

Focusing on the Facts

1. What are some indicators that Jesus is God (see pp. 28-29)?
2. Give some examples from Christ's life that indicate He was human (see p. 29).
3. Why did Jesus come into the world (see p. 29)?
4. What verdict did Pilate's wife render concerning Jesus (Matt. 27:19; see p. 34)?
5. Why was Pilate's wife afraid (see p. 34)?
6. What Old Testament teaching might Pilate have been trying to follow when he washed his hands in front of the multitude in Matthew 27:24 (see p. 36)?
7. Why does God establish capital punishment in Genesis 9:6 (see p. 36)?

8. Explain the process of scourging (see p. 37).
9. What happened to Jesus after He was scourged (John 19:2-3; see pp. 37-38)?
10. Why did Pilate display Jesus before the crowd after he had had Him scourged? What effect did that have (see p. 38)?
11. Why does Pilate become more afraid in John 19:8 (see p. 39)?

Pondering the Principles

1. Review the introductory section about Christ (see pp. 28-32). Record the five attributes of Christ that have meant the most to you in your Christian life. Meditate on one each day during your quiet time next week. Use that time to grow ever closer to your Savior. Make it a time of offering special reverence and worship to Him.

2. The trials of Jesus Christ proved His innocence and exposed the guilt of His accusers and executors. Where do you stand? Are you aligned with the spotless Lamb of God, or are you still guilty as a result of your rejection of Him? If you haven't accepted the death of Christ on your behalf, you still can make that choice. But remember, by not making a choice you have made a choice (Matt. 12:30). You have chosen to reject Him. Please consider the opportunity you have at this moment. Don't let it pass by without confronting your sin and giving it to the One who can take it away.

3
The Wickedness of the Crucifixion—Part 1

Outline

Introduction
A. The Viewpoint of John
B. The Viewpoint of Matthew
   1. The triumph of wickedness
   2. The torment of wickedness

Lesson
 I. The Ignorant Wicked—The Callous Soldiers (vv. 27-37)
  A. The Mockery of Jesus (vv. 27-30)
    1. The guilt of Pilate (v. 27)
     a) The sin of Pilate
     b) The soldiers of Pilate
      (1) Their identification
      (2) Their ignorance
     c) The supervision of Pilate
    2. The game of the soldiers (vv. 28-30)
     a) The stripping of the King (v. 28*a*)
     b) The symbols of the King (vv. 28*b*-29)
      (1) The robe (v. 28*b*)
       (*a*) Purple
       (*b*) Scarlet
      (2) The crown (v. 29*a*)
      (3) The scepter (v. 29*b*)
     c) The suffering of the King (vv. 29*c*-30)
      (1) Mocking His royalty (vv. 29*c*-30*a*)
      (2) Mocking His authority (v. 30*b*)

B. The Crucifixion of Jesus (vv. 31-37)
   1. The plan (v. 31)
   2. The pilgrimage (vv. 32-33)
      a) Inside the city (v. 32a)
         (1) The definition of the cross
         (2) The display of the criminal
         (3) The dissipation of Christ
      b) Outside the city (v. 32b)
         (1) The provision of Simon
            (a) His residence
            (b) His conscription
            (c) His family
            (d) His salvation
         (2) The place of the skull (v. 33)
   3. The preparation (v. 34)
      a) The sedative offered (v. 34a)
         (1) Its purpose
         (2) Its provision
      b) The sedative refused (v. 34b)
   4. The profits (v. 35)
   5. The protectors (v. 36)
   6. The pronouncement (v. 37)

Introduction

Many years ago, scholar Frederic Farrar wrote *The Life of Christ* (New York: A. L. Burt, 1874). In it he said this:

"A death by crucifixion seems to include all that pain and death can have of horrible and ghastly—dizziness, cramp, thirst, starvation, sleeplessness, traumatic fever, tetanus, shame, publicity of shame, long continuance of torment, horror of anticipation, mortification of untended wounds—all intensified just up to the point at which they can be endured at all, but all stopping just short of the point which would give to the sufferer the relief of unconsciousness.

"The unnatural position made every movement painful; the lacerated veins and crushed tendons throbbed with incessant anguish; the wounds, inflamed by exposure, gradually gangrened; the arteries—especially of the head and stomach—became swollen and oppressed with surcharged blood; and while each variety of misery went on gradually increasing, there was added to them the intolerable pang of burning and raging thirst, and all these physical complications caused an internal excitement and anxiety, which made the prospect of death itself—of death, the awful unknown enemy, at whose approach man usually shudders most—bear the aspect of a delicious and exquisite release" (p. 499).

One thing is clear: first-century executions were not like modern ones. The authorities did not seek a quick, painless death to preserve a small measure of dignity for the criminal. On the contrary, they sought an agonizing torture to completely humiliate him. Such was the torture that our Lord Jesus Christ endured for us.

The crucifixion of Christ is the climax of redemptive history. God's plan of salvation culminates in the cross, as the Lord bears the sins of the world and provides salvation for all who believe in Him.

A. The Viewpoint of John

The cross demonstrates the grace, mercy, goodness, kindness, and love of God like no other event in history ever can. We could go to Scripture and focus entirely on God's self-revelation of love and grace in the cross. That is, for the most part, the intention of the gospel of John. He looked at the cross from the viewpoint of God. He revealed that it is the fulfillment of prophecy—that God's plan is on schedule. As you read John's record of the crucifixion, you cannot help but be in awe at the wonder of God's glory, grace, and love in the death of Jesus Christ.

B. The Viewpoint of Matthew

Matthew approached the cross from the opposite perspective. He showed how the death of Jesus Christ demonstrated the wickedness of the human heart.

When Peter preaches his sermon on the Day of Pentecost in Acts 2:22-23, he says that God has ordained Christ's death but that the wicked hands of the people have brought it to pass. Jeremiah 17:9 says, "The heart is deceitful above all things, and desperately wicked." If ever there was a place where we could see that verse proved, it was at the crucifixion of Christ.

47

1. The triumph of wickedness

    It is not as if wickedness had not appeared previously in the life of Christ. It tried to kill Him at birth. It tried to discredit His teaching and stop His miracles. Wickedness secured His condemnation by violating every standard of justice in the Jewish and Gentile world. It betrayed Him by the kiss of a hypocrite. It had Him arrested. It framed Him, slapped His face, punched Him, spit on Him, scourged Him, and mocked Him. Yet before it is through, wickedness will kill Him.

2. The torment of wickedness

    However, even death itself wasn't enough to satiate its evil desire—it had to torment Him as well. It had to mock, scorn, and reproach Him until He breathed His last. Christ's enemies were so filled with wickedness that His death seemed to be a disappointment to them. They would have wished to prolong it so they could continue spewing their venom on Him. The heartless intensity of the words and deeds of all who surrounded the cross cannot adequately be described.

    Matthew described four groups of wicked people at the cross: the ignorant wicked, the knowing wicked, the fickle wicked, and the religious wicked.

Lesson

I. THE IGNORANT WICKED—THE CALLOUS SOLDIERS (vv. 27-37)

    A. The Mockery of Jesus (vv. 27-30)

        1. The guilt of Pilate (v. 27)

            "Then the soldiers of the governor [Pilate] took Jesus into the common hall [praetorium], and gathered unto him the whole band of soldiers."

48

a) The sin of Pilate

Pilate had already violated justice, conscience, conviction, truth, integrity, and character. He sold his soul for popularity and security. When he was cornered by the Jewish population, the security of his position was in jeopardy. He was fearful that another insurrection from the Jews would result in the loss of his job and reputation. He felt forced into doing things to Jesus he knew weren't just. Instead of releasing Jesus, who he repeatedly pronounced innocent, he tried to satiate the mob's thirst for blood by scourging and mocking Him. He then tried to present Christ as a pathetic individual who couldn't possibly be a threat to Rome or Israel. He hoped this strategy would cause the crowd to stop short of forcing him to execute an innocent man.

b) The soldiers of Pilate

As we begin our study, Jesus had already endured the scourging (Matt. 27:26; see pp. 37-38). Following the scourging but before the crucifixion, the scene in verse 27 took place. Jesus was taken to the common hall, and the whole band was gathered around Him. The Greek word translated "whole band" is *speira* and refers to 600 soldiers.

(1) Their identification

These soldiers were Roman legionnaires who, for the most part, were not Italian. Acts 10:1 says Cornelius was in the Italian band, but that was not the norm. Rome generally conscripted soldiers out of the countries it occupied. In Israel the Romans frequently used Syrian soldiers because they could speak Aramaic, which was the common language of Israel. The majority of Rome's soldiers were not necessarily Roman, but they reflected Roman military power and presence. The Jews were exempt from service in the Roman military, and they wouldn't have served even if they could.

(2) Their ignorance

This particular band that surrounded Christ was under Pilate, whose headquarters were at Caesarea on the seacoast, about sixty miles west of Jerusalem. They were probably not familiar with Jerusalem and its religion. They certainly didn't understand much about Jesus, if they even understood anything at all. So what they did was out of ignorance. He was just a prisoner to them, and a curious one at that. It wasn't often that they got to meet prisoners who claimed to be king.

The soldiers would have seen Jesus as a strange and pathetic figure. His face had been slapped and punched until it was swollen and bruised. He had been spit on. His body had been lacerated, and He was bleeding profusely from the shoulders down. They knew He claimed to be a king from what the people screamed about Him. They also knew the people wanted Him dead. So they saw Him as a fake and a fraud, thinking He was mentally deranged and worthy of their mockery. Yet throughout His encounter with them, Jesus never said a thing. The soldiers treated Him like a clown, as they would have treated a poor idiot boy in the street. They were cold, indifferent, and ignorant.

c) The supervision of Pilate

Under the tutelage of Pilate, the soldiers mocked Jesus' claim to be a king. I do not believe the soldiers did this independently of Pilate; I think they did it under his watchful eye. John 19:4 tells us that when Jesus was brought out to the crowd after the scourging, Pilate "went forth again." So he must have been in the praetorium, aware of what was happening. I'm sure he looked on it with favor because he wanted Jesus to appear as a mock king. Then he could confront the Jews about their claim that He was a threat to Rome or Israel.

2. The game of the soldiers (vv. 28-30)

Already bleeding and in agony from the scourging, Jesus became the object of ridicule as the soldiers began their game. They didn't do it reluctantly. They hated the Jews. They would thoroughly enjoy any opportunity they might have to mock them. Jesus had never done anything to them. Yet they had no interest in alleviating His agony. They showed no concern for His suffering and no interest in healing His wounds. They were bent on aggravating that agony. They had been trained to torture and kill, so they were thirsty for blood. They reflected the heart of their father the devil, who is a roaring lion seeking whom he may devour (1 Pet. 5:8).

a) The stripping of the King (v. 28a)

"And they stripped him."

When Jesus was scourged, He was naked. After the scourging was complete, the soldiers put Jesus' inner robe back on Him. One can only imagine the pain that rough cloth would have caused when put over His open wounds. He had worn it for some time before He was brought back into the praetorium. As the soldiers began their game, they heartlessly ripped that robe off Him once more, again exposing His wounds.

b) The symbols of the King (vv. 28b-29)

(1) The robe (v. 28b)

"And put on him a scarlet robe."

The soldiers found a discarded scarlet robe—a robe that one of the soldiers would have worn as an outer garment—and put it on Jesus. Matthew said it was scarlet in color; John said it was purple (John 19:2). There must be a reason for that.

(*a*) Purple

John may have seen it as purple because that color represents majesty. That would give greater emphasis to the soldiers' treatment of Jesus as a mock king.

(*b*) Scarlet

Isaiah 1:18 says, "Though your sins be as scarlet." Matthew may have seen the robe as the symbol of our sins. Jesus bore our sins. He who knew no sin became sin for us (2 Cor. 5:21).

(2) The crown (v. 29*a*)

"When they had plaited a crown [Gk., *stephanos*] of thorns [Gk., *akantha*], they put it upon his head."

We don't know what plant the thorns came from. The soldiers intended the crown to be a cheap and painful imitation of the wreath worn by Tiberius Caesar. Verse 29 says the soldiers put it (Gk., *epithitemi*) around His head, no doubt crushing it down around His head. The thorns pierced His brow and little streams of blood would have run down His face.

I am reminded of Genesis 3:18. After the sin of Adam and Eve, God cursed the earth and said, "Thorns also and thistles shall it bring forth." I see the crown as a symbol of His bearing the curse of the world. Jesus not only took away sin on the cross but removed the curse of the whole earth as well. Romans 8:19 says the whole creation waits "for the manifestation of the sons of God." It too shall be liberated from the curse.

(3) The scepter (v. 29*b*)

"[They put] a reed in his right hand."

The right hand is the symbol of authority. The reed symbolized a king's scepter. It was a common stalk. The soldiers put it in His hand to mock Christ's authority. On Roman coins, the image of Tiberius was shown holding a scepter.

c) The suffering of the King (vv. 29*c*-30)

(1) Mocking His royalty (vv. 29*c*-30*a*)

"They bowed the knee before him, and mocked him, saying, Hail, King of the Jews! And they spat upon him."

There was no sincerity in that proclamation, only sarcasm and ridicule. In Matthew 26:68 the Jewish leaders mock His claim to be a prophet.

The ultimate human indignity is to be spit upon. The Jewish leaders had spit on Him (Matt. 26:67), and now the Roman soldiers were doing so.

(2) Mocking His authority (v. 30*b*)

"And took the reed, and smote him on the head."

The soldiers hit His head repeatedly with the reed. Why? To make a joke of His authority. What kind of a king could He possibly be if they could rip His scepter out of His hand and beat Him on the head with it? Christ's sovereignty was a joke to them. They thought if they could spit on Him and hit Him in the head with his own scepter, and have nothing happen in retaliation, then He couldn't be a king.

The mockery of Jesus was a display of unbelievable human evil. The soldiers had nothing against Christ; they were reveling in the depravity of their hearts in their brutal amusement. Yet through it all Jesus endured. He said nothing, offered no resistance. He was willing to suffer for sinners—not only the death on the cross but everything that came with it as well. Hebrews 12:3 says He "endured such contradiction of sinners against himself." He endured it because He knew it was going to happen. Earlier told His disciples, "We go up to Jerusalem; and the Son of man shall be betrayed unto the chief priests and unto the scribes, and they shall condemn him to death, and shall deliver him to the Gentiles to mock, and to scourge, and to crucify him. And the third day he shall rise again" (Matt. 20:18-19). Jesus was right on schedule. He had been to the Jews; now He was with the Gentiles. And He remained silent despite the humiliation and agony.

B. The Crucifixion of Jesus (vv. 31-37)

Matthew skips over what happened immediately after the mockery, but John 19:2-15 tells us (see pp. 37-41).

1. The plan (v. 31)

"After they had mocked him, they took the robe off from him, and put his own raiment on him, and led him away to crucify him."

Commentator William Barclay tells us that crucifixion "originated in Persia; and its origin came from the fact that the earth was considered to be sacred to Ormuzd, the god, and the criminal was lifted up from it that he might not defile the earth, which was God's property. From Persia, crucifixion passed to Carthage in North Africa; and it was from Carthage that Rome learned it" (*The Gospel of Matthew*, vol. 2 [Philadelphia: Westminster, 1975], p. 365). The Romans used crucifixion extensively. At the time of Christ and during the era of Roman occupation in Israel, the Romans crucified at least thirty thousand Jews. It was carried out along the highways to warn people of what happens to someone who violates Roman law. Crucifixion was a vivid illustration of the consequences of opposing Rome.

2. The pilgrimage (vv. 32-33)

   a) Inside the city (v. 32a)

   "As they came out."

   The soldiers were going to lead a victim to crucifixion, so they followed the normal procedure.
   Matthew skips over some things that happened before they left the city. Executions had to take place
   out of the city because the Jews didn't want it to be
   defiled (e.g., Lev. 4:12). Hebrews 13:12 says that Jesus "suffered outside the gate."

   We do need to understand what happened to Jesus
   after He was led from the praetorium but before He
   left the city.

   (1) The definition of the cross

       John 19:16-17 says, "Then delivered he him,
       therefore, unto them to be crucified. And they
       took Jesus, and led him away. And he, bearing
       his cross, went forth." We know that Jesus began
       the procession by carrying His cross. There is
       nothing in Scripture to suggest that Jesus carried
       only a part of the cross. Some think He carried
       just the crosspiece, and some think He carried the
       centerpiece. I believe He carried the whole thing.
       The cross would have weighed in excess of two
       hundred pounds. That was an incredible weight
       for someone in His condition to carry.

   (2) The display of the criminal

       The procession would have gone like this: the
       prisoner would be surrounded by four Roman
       soldiers, one at each corner, moving Him
       through the city, with other soldiers before and
       behind. Jerusalem was swelling with pilgrims
       who had come to worship and celebrate the Pass-
       over. And since this was the day of the Passover,
       the city would have been crawling with people.
       The soldiers would parade the prisoner down the

main streets. Either hanging from the prisoner's neck, or held by someone walking in front, was a placard explaining why the prisoner was to be executed. In that way, the people would know the price of that particular crime.

Jesus' Last Public Lesson

During His procession through the streets of Jerusalem, Jesus gave His last public lesson, and it was a brief one.

1. The lesson

Luke 23:27-29 says, "There followed him a great company of people, and of women, who also bewailed and lamented him. But Jesus, turning unto them, said, Daughters of Jerusalem, weep not for me, but weep for yourselves, and for your children. For, behold, the days are coming, in which they shall say, Blessed are the barren, and the wombs that never bore, and the breasts which never nursed." That is something no Jewish mother could ever imagine being said. Yet there was a day coming when they would wish they had no children. Jesus also said, "Then shall they begin to say to the mountains, Fall on us; and to the hills, Cover us" (v. 30). There was coming such terrifying judgment that they would wish they didn't have children because they were going to see them slaughtered.

2. The proverb

Jesus continued with the following proverb: "For if they do these things in a green tree, what shall be done in the dry?" (v. 31). Now what did He mean by that? Jesus was the green tree, and the populace of Jerusalem was the dry one. If the Romans would crucify Him, an innocent man, what would they do to the Jewish nation, which was guilty? Because Jesus was a green tree, He should not have been considered as fuel for burning. But since the nation was dry, it should have been burned. You burn dry wood, not green wood. If the Romans would kill an innocent man, what would they do to the guilty, who continued to initiate insurrections against the Romans? Of course Jesus was referring to the destruction of Jerusalem in A.D. 70, which was precipitated by their hostilities against Rome.

Jesus' last message to the people was of coming judgment. And that judgment came quickly, within the lifetime of many of the people. The land of Israel has yet to recover.

In Matthew 27:32 the procession comes out of the city through the northern gate along the main highway. Executions occurred along the main highways so the people passing by would have agonizing testimony to the consequences of violating Rome.

(3) The dissipation of Christ

As the procession came out of the city, it was apparent that Jesus' strength was giving out. I believe He was the strongest man who ever lived because He was without sin. There was no defilement in His body; therefore it would have been all that God intended an undefiled body to be. Yet even given that, Jesus' strength ran out. His blood was draining away. The agony He endured is beyond belief. Up to now He had no sleep since the night before. He had been betrayed by Judas and witnessed the defection of His disciples. He had undergone the injustice of His trials and endured the humiliations that followed. The scourgings and beatings had taxed His strength. There were no angels to strengthen Him as they had after the forty days of fasting and temptation in the wilderness (Matt. 4:1-11).

b) Outside the city (v. 32b)

"They found a man of Cyrene, Simon by name; him they compelled to bear his cross."

(1) The provision of Simon

(a) His residence

Cyrene was a Greek settlement located west of Alexandria and directly south of Greece on the north African coast, about ten miles inland—in modern-day Libya. Many Jews lived there because it was a center of trade. Simon no doubt was in Jerusalem because of the Passover. We do know that there was a Jewish synagogue for Cyrenians in Jerusalem (Acts 6:9). We believe he was Jewish, because Simon is a Jewish name.

(b) His conscription

Mark 15:21 says, "They compel one Simon, of Cyrene, who passed by, coming out of the country." As Jesus came out of the city, Simon was coming out of the country. We don't know why he was walking in the country. He may have been visiting someone, or perhaps he was securing some things in preparation for the Passover. Some have suggested that he shouldn't have been out walking on a holy day. But the Sabbath law didn't necessarily apply on a feast day, only on a Sabbath day. So it was fine for him to be out walking. As he walked by the procession, he was conscripted by the Roman soldiers to carry the cross of Jesus. No Roman would carry a criminal's cross —and certainly not that of a Jewish criminal.

(c) His family

Mark 15:21 says that Simon was "the father of Alexander and Rufus." Alexander and Rufus are Greek names. So Simon, a Jewish man, gave his sons Greek names. That was not an unusual practice; it was quite common, especially for someone living in a region other than Israel.

Why did Mark identify Alexander and Rufus? Because Mark probably wrote his gospel from Rome, and his first readers may well have belonged to the Roman church. It is likely that they knew Alexander and Rufus. The apostle Paul said, "Greet Rufus, chosen in the Lord, and his mother and mine" (Rom. 16:13). Who would the mother of Rufus be? The wife of Simon.

(*d*) His salvation

It's not difficult to imagine that Simon, although inadvertently passing by and being made to carry the cross of Jesus Christ, came to Christ through that experience and raised two sons who became pillars in the church at Rome. Evidently his wife became like a mother to the apostle Paul. So what began as an enforced act may well have been the means of a family's conversion. I like to think that when we get to heaven we're going to meet Simon of Cyrene, along with his wife and children.

(2) The place of the skull (v. 33)

"When they were come unto a place called Golgotha, that is to say, a place of a skull."

Golgotha is an Aramaic term transliterated into Greek and then into English. It means "skull place." Luke used the Greek word *kranion*, from which we get "cranium" (Luke 23:33). The Latin Vulgate translates that "Calvary," which is the Latin word for "cranium."

Some have suggested it was a place where skulls were lying on the ground. But that would mean it should have been called the place of the skulls. Furthermore, you can be sure that the Jews wouldn't allow bones to lie around. It was called the place of a skull because it was shaped like that. I have visited a place in Jerusalem that is believed to be that very spot. It still looks like a skull. It is located right outside the north part of Jerusalem along the main highway.

3. The preparation (v. 34)

   a) The sedative offered (v. 34*a*)

   "They gave him vinegar to drink, mingled with gall."

   (1) Its purpose

   The Greek text indicates that they gave Him wine (Gk., *oinos*) to drink. Gall is a general term referring to something bitter. Mark 15:23 says that myrrh was mixed with the wine. Myrrh is a bitter gum resin that was put into the wine as a way of calming a person (cf. Ps. 69:21). In the first century A.D. it was thought to have narcotic properties (Dioscorides Pedanius, *Materia Medica*, I.lxiv.3).

   The soldiers didn't look on the drugging of the victim as an act of mercy; they didn't care if the victim suffered or not. The drugging accommodated them because it might have been difficult to hammer four nails through someone's limbs if he weren't drugged to some degree. Consequently, it was helpful for them to have some way to drug their victim.

   (2) Its provision

   According to tradition, an association of wealthy women in Jerusalem provided gall to ease the pain of victims (cf. Babylonian Talmud *Sanhedrin* 43*a*). They did that to fulfill Proverbs 31:6: "Give strong drink unto him that is ready to perish, and wine unto those that are of heavy hearts."

   b) The sedative refused (v. 34*b*)

   "When he had tasted it, he would not drink."

   Jesus wouldn't drink the mixture of wine and myrrh. Why? Because He said earlier, "The cup which my Father hath given me, shall I not drink it?" (John 18:11). He was not going to allow any of His senses to be dulled. He was committed to enduring the full pain of the cross.

4. The profits (v. 35)

"They crucified him, and parted his garments, casting lots."

Matthew uses no dramatic adjectives to describe the pain. He simply says, "They crucified him."

The Preoccupation of Scripture

As I looked at Matthew 27:35, I thought perhaps the English translation missed something. So I examined the Greek text and discovered that its treatment is even less graphic than the English text. The Greek text literally says, "The having-crucified-Him-ones parted His garments." The crucifixion is referred to offhandedly only as a way to describe the ones who parted Christ's garments. Why does Matthew not go into more detail? Because his point is the wickedness of the men. Matthew is not preoccupied with the physical agony of Jesus on the cross; it is preoccupied with the wickedness of men. It doesn't describe the agony of Jesus; it only describes what men did to Him. Outside of what Christ endured in the Garden of Gethsemane (Luke 22:44), we know nothing of His agony. Even His words while on the cross do not express His physical agony, only His separation from God.

A Scribal Addition

Matthew 27:35 in the King James Version adds the following prophecy: "That it might be fulfilled which was spoken by the prophet, They parted my garments among them, and upon my vesture did they cast lots." That is a quote from Psalm 22:18. But that prophecy doesn't belong in Matthew 27:35. It was most likely borrowed from John 19:24. It is not in the oldest manuscripts of Matthew. What probably happened was that a scribe copying Matthew remembered the prophecy from John 19:24 and added it in the margin of Matthew, just like the verses you find in the margins of an annotated Bible. Later, another scribe copying the same section might have thought the prophecy should be included in the text, removed it from the margin, and entered it into the text. You can see why it is important to search out the oldest manuscripts.

All that doesn't make the prophecy any less true. Matthew 27:35 is a fulfillment of Psalm 22:18. The apostle John made a point of recording fulfilled prophecy because he was looking at the cross from God's viewpoint. However, Matthew left out such references because he was concerned about showing the wickedness of men.

Matthew said that Jesus' crucifiers parted His garments—they divided them up. A Jewish man usually wore five pieces of clothing: shoes, an inner garment, a headpiece, belt, and outer cloak. The soldiers each took one piece and, according to John 19:23, the inner garment remained. It was a seamless garment that had holes for the arms and head. Since there were four soldiers, they decided to gamble for the inner garment by casting lots. That was a fulfillment of Psalm 22:18, but Matthew didn't comment on it. He wanted us to see how indifferent the soldiers were.

5. The protectors (v. 36)

"Sitting down they watched him there."

Why did they sit and watch Jesus? It was their job. They were on guard in case someone tried to be unduly savage to Christ or in case someone tried to rescue Him. With cruel mockery they stayed on their guard to make sure nothing happened beyond what had already happened.

6. The pronouncement (v. 37)

"And set up over his head his accusation written, THIS IS JESUS, THE KING OF THE JEWS."

Comparing Matthew, Mark, Luke, and John gives us the complete statement: "THIS IS JESUS OF NAZARETH, THE KING OF THE JEWS." The Jewish leaders didn't like that. In John 19:21 they tell Pilate to change the wording. But Pilate said, "What I have written, I have written" (John 19:22). Pilate was mocking the leaders. He wanted the people to look at that claim and laugh at both Jesus and the Jewish nation. He even had it written in three languages: Greek, the universal language; Aramaic, the language of the area; and Latin, the language of the Romans. Pilate remained sarcastic to the end.

The world is full of people who are like the soldiers. Many people laugh at even the thought of Jesus, seeing Him as a joke. The world is full of ignorant people who are callous toward Jesus Christ. They don't know who it is they are rejecting. Unless they awaken to Him, they'll spend an eternity with the same kind of remorse these soldiers are experiencing now.

However, there is a beautiful ending to this scene. Matthew 27:54 says, "When the centurion [a commander of 100 soldiers], and they that were with him watching Jesus, saw the earthquake, and those things that were done, they feared greatly, saying, Truly, this was the Son of God." Luke 23:47 says, "When the centurion saw what was done, he glorified God, saying, Certainly this was a righteous man." Out of that group of soldiers at least one came to true faith in Christ. As Jesus hung dying on the cross, put there by ignorant, wicked men, He made the salvation He was procuring for all men available to His crucifiers. Is He not the friend of sinners?

Focusing on the Facts

1. What viewpoint did John emphasize in his record of the crucifixion? What viewpoint did Matthew emphasize (see p. 47)?
2. What effect did wickedness have on Christ throughout His life (see p. 48)?
3. How many soldiers gathered around Christ in the common hall? Who were they (Matt. 27:27; see p. 49)?
4. Why can we assume this group of soldiers was ignorant of Jesus (see p. 50)?
5. What is one possible reason that Matthew and John used different colors to describe the robe the soldiers put on Jesus (Matt. 27:28; see pp. 51-52)?
6. What did the crown of thorns symbolize (Matt. 27:29; see p. 52)?
7. What did the reed symbolize (Matt. 27:29; see p. 53)?

8. What characteristics of Jesus did the soldiers mock (Matt. 27:29-30; see p. 53)?
9. Why did Jesus endure such severe treatment in silence (see p. 54)?
10. Why did the Romans crucify their victims alongside the highways (see p. 54)?
11. Why did executions have to take place outside the city (see p. 55)?
12. Describe the procession that led Jesus to the cross (see pp. 55-56)?
13. What did Jesus teach the people about as He was being led to the cross? What did the proverb describe (Luke 23:27-31; see pp. 56-57)?
14. Who was Simon? Why was it ultimately significant that he was chosen to carry the cross of Christ (Matt. 27:32; see pp. 57-59)?
15. Describe the location where Christ was crucified. What does Calvary mean (Matt. 27:33; see p. 59)?
16. What was the purpose for giving Christ a mixture of wine and myrrh to drink? Who provided this mixture for the soldiers (see p. 60)?
17. Why did Jesus refuse to drink the wine mixture (see pp. 60-61)?
18. Why didn't Matthew go into more detail in describing the crucifixion (see p. 61)?
19. Why did the soldiers sit down and watch Jesus while He hung on the cross (see p. 62)?

Pondering the Principles

1. We have seen that the crucifixion of Christ was one great example of Jeremiah 17:9, which says, "The heart is deceitful above all things, and desperately wicked." What is on the inside of man—not the outside—is what is most important to God. Look up the following verses: 1 Samuel 16:7; 1 Chronicles 28:9; Psalm 44:20-21; 139:1-4; and Hebrews 4:12. What is God able to see when He looks at any man? What would God see if He were to look inside you? If there are things He can see in your life that you wish He couldn't, take this time to confess them before God. Pour out all the evil you have been holding in your heart. Ask Him to reveal to you any evil that you might store in your heart in the future. Now thank God that He loves you so much that He is willing to relieve you of the burden and guilt of sin.

2. Review the section on the mocking of Jesus (see pp. 48-54). How do you think you would respond if put in similar circumstances? Read 1 Peter 2:21-25. What have you learned from Christ's attitude toward those who mocked Him? How can you apply the things you have learned to situations you face today?

3. There are many people who fall into the category of the ignorant wicked. You may even know some of them. Has your perception of those people changed as a result of this study? How might you approach them about the claims of Christ? Remember, although you are not of this world, you are still in it. That means you cannot avoid associating with the ungodly to some degree. Just be sure that when you do, you present the claims of Christ to them.

4
The Wickedness of the Crucifixion—Part 2

Outline

Introduction
A. The Expression of the World's Wickedness
B. The Extent of Christ's Sufferings

Review
  I. The Ignorant Wicked—The Callous Soldiers (vv. 27-37)
     A. The Mockery of Jesus (vv. 27-30)
     B. The Crucifixion of Jesus (vv. 31-37)

Lesson
 II. The Knowing Wicked—The Crass Thieves (vv. 38, 44)
     A. Their Character (v. 38)
     B. Their Contempt (v. 44)
III. The Fickle Wicked—The Careless Crowd (vv. 39-40)
     A. Their Decreasing Enthusiasm (v. 39a)
     B. Their Increasing Rejection (vv. 39b-40)
        1. Physical taunting (v. 39b)
        2. Verbal taunting (v. 40)
           a) The claims
              (1) He would raise the Temple
              (2) He claimed to be the Son of God
           b) The challenge
           c) The conviction
 IV. The Religious Wicked—The Cruel Leaders (vv. 41-43)
     A. The Hypocritical Authorities (v. 41)
     B. The Hateful Attacks (vv. 42-43)
        1. Against Christ's Power (v. 42)
           a) His healing ministry (v. 42a)
           b) His sovereignty (v. 42b)
        2. Against Christ's person (v. 43)

Conclusion
A. The Guilty
   1. Zechariah 12:10
   2. Hebrews 6:6
B. The Forgiven
   1. A centurion
   2. A thief
   3. A crowd
   4. A company of priests

Introduction

Jesus clearly stated that His generation was wicked (Matt. 16:4). He said the leaders of Israel were full of wickedness (Matt. 22:18; Luke 11:39). Paul, in reference to unbelieving Christ-rejectors, said they are filled with all wickedness (Rom. 1:29). The heart of man is desperately wicked (Jer. 17:9). When given over to his own devices, man will perpetrate crimes beyond imagination.

A. The Expression of the World's Wickedness

The wickedness of man is clearly seen in the execution of Jesus Christ. Nothing could prove more conclusively the pervasive corruption of human nature. That seems to be Matthew's particular concern in writing his gospel. As we go through Matthew's record of the crucifixion, we see unrelenting evil.

Commentator David Thomas wrote, "For six thousand years wickedness had been growing. It had wrought deeds of impiety and crime that had rung the ages with agony, and often roused the justice of the universe to roll her fiery thunderbolts of retribution through the world. But now it had grown to full maturity; it stands around the cross in such gigantic proportions as had never been seen before; it works an enormity before which the mightiest of its past exploits dwindle into insignificance and pale into dimness. It crucifies the Lord of life and glory" (*The Gospel of Matthew: A Homiletical Commentary* [Grand Rapids: Kregel, 1979], p. 536).

B. The Extent of Christ's Sufferings

Wicked men were not content just to execute Jesus Christ; they had to torment Him in the process. Such is the cruelty of the human heart when fully exposed.

We should not be shocked at the sorrow our Savior bore. He was a man of sorrows (Isa. 53:3). His sufferings were great. They were too great even for us to comprehend fully. We could say He suffered more sorrow than any man who ever lived. According to Isaiah 53:4, He bore our griefs and carried our sorrows. So, in bearing sin, Jesus bore the collective grief and sorrow of every person who ever lived. He also experienced sorrow at being alienated and separated from His Father for a time as He bore the sins of the world. Jesus suffered more than all men put together have ever suffered.

The prophet Isaiah said the Messiah was acquainted with grief (Isa. 53:3). He experienced little else. Grief was His constant companion. He wept on several occasions, but never does Scripture indicate that He laughed. Many Christians centuries ago used to beg God to give them mercy for the unknown sufferings they might have caused Jesus Christ. They realized they could not even conceive of all the suffering He endured.

How Did Christ Suffer?

1. He suffered from temptation

Hebrews 4:15 says He "was in all points tempted like as we are, yet without sin." Hebrews 2:18 says, "He himself hath suffered being tempted." Jesus was constantly assaulted by temptation. His temptation was real even though He never sinned.

2. He suffered from self-denial

Jesus refused to have what we assume to be the normal comforts of life. He deprived Himself. As Henry Barraclough said in his hymn "Ivory Palaces," our Lord went "out of the ivory palaces, into a world of woe." Paul said Christ "thought it not robbery to be equal with God, but made himself of no reputation, and took upon him the form of a servant, and was made in the likeness of men; and, being found in fashion as a man, he humbled himself and became obedient unto death" (Phil. 2:6-8). He was born in a stable. He had no personal possessions. He experienced hunger, thirst, weariness, and the absence of all worldly comforts.

3. He suffered from rejection

Jesus was hated, despised, mocked, maligned, reviled, rebuked, blasphemed, reproached, and falsely accused. All that reached a furious culmination in the events around His cross.

4. He suffered from sin

Although He was sinless, Jesus bore all the sins of all the world on the cross. Paul said Jesus actually became sin for us (2 Cor. 5:21). He suffered from the weight of sin. And because of His omniscience, He no doubt suffered in anticipation of His suffering.

5. He suffered from Satan

Satan plagued Jesus from the time of His birth, having tried to eliminate Him by Herod's decree. He continued his assault on Jesus in the Garden of Gethsemane with three great waves of temptation in an attempt to dissuade Him from going to the cross. Satan threw all the fury of hell on Jesus' head, yet he could only bruise His heel (Gen. 3:15). Yet that still caused Jesus tremendous suffering. Satan used even His beloved Peter to tempt Him. Jesus had to say, "Get thee behind me, Satan" (Matt. 16:23). In one final assault, the devil entered Judas and used him to betray Christ.

6. He suffered from the wrath of God

When Jesus became sin on the cross, God poured out on Him all of heaven's fury against all the sin on earth.

Matthew 27:27-44 shows us Christ's suffering at the hands of wicked men. Matthew's objective was to emphasize the rejection of the

King. And that rejection mounted until it reached its climax in the crucifixion. To help us see the wickedness of the scene, I want to draw your attention to four different groups: the ignorant wicked, the knowing wicked, the fickle wicked, and the religious wicked. Every person in the world who does not come to faith in Jesus Christ fits into one of those groups. They were all present at the cross, and they are still around today.

Review

I. THE IGNORANT WICKED—THE CALLOUS SOLDIERS (vv. 27-37; see pp. 48-63)

    A. The Mockery of Jesus (vv. 27-30; see pp. 48-54)

The Return of the King

As the Roman soldiers mocked Christ's sovereignty, little did they know He was a king who one day would wear a different blood-spattered robe. Revelation 19:13 shows Jesus Christ coming out of heaven in glory wearing a robe of majesty. However, this robe will be spotted with the blood of His enemies and not with His own blood. One day Jesus will also wear a royal crown (Gk., *diadema*) far different from a crown of thorns (Gk., *stephanos*). In fact, Revelation 19:12 says He will wear many crowns. Jesus alone will be King. Some day He will wield a scepter, but it will not be a reed. According to Revelation 19:15, Jesus will rule with a rod of iron, with which He will bring instant judgment on an unbelieving world. There will be no one to mock Jesus then. Psalm 2:4 says, "He who sitteth in the heavens shall laugh; the Lord shall have them in derision."

    B. The Crucifixion of Jesus (vv. 31-37; see pp. 54-63)

Examining a Crucifixion

Matthew doesn't give the details of the crucifixion, but it is helpful to have some understanding of what Christ endured on the cross. The soldiers first laid the cross on the ground and then placed Him on it. They extended His feet, pulling His toes down. Then they drove a large nail through the arch of one foot and then through the arch of the other foot. Next, they extended His hands, allowing His knees to flex a little. Then they drove two great nails through His wrists, just below the heel of each hand. They couldn't put them through the palms because the flesh would tear.

Once the soldiers nailed Christ to the cross, they lifted it and dropped it into a hole. When it hit bottom, the shock caused Him great pain. He was now crucified. Slowly He began to sag down more and more. With His weight being held by the nails running through His wrists, excruciating pain shot up His arms. To try to relieve the pain, the Lord pushed up on the two wounds in His feet. That caused even more pain. Hour after hour He endured a wrenching, twisting trade-off as He tried to relieve the pain in His hands and then in His feet. After a while, the pain made it impossible to move.

Dr. Truman Davis writes,

"At this point, another phenomenon occurred as the arms fatigued: great waves of cramps sweep over the muscles knotting them in deep, relentless, throbbing pain. With these cramps comes the inability to push Himself upward. Hanging by His arms, the pectoral muscles are paralyzed and the intercostal muscles are unable to act. Air can be drawn into the lungs but it can't be exhaled. Jesus fights to raise Himself to get even one short breath. Finally carbon dioxide builds up in the lungs and in the blood stream and the cramps subside. He would grasp short breaths of air, [experience] hours of limitless pain, cycles of twisting joint-rending cramps, intermittent partial asphyxiation, searing pain as tissue is torn from His lacerated back as He moves up and down the rough timber, a deep crushing pain in the chest as the pericardium slowly fills with [fluid] and begins to compress the heart. And this leads to death."

What agony!

Lesson

II. THE KNOWING WICKED—THE CRASS THIEVES (vv. 38, 44)

A. Their Character (v. 38)

"Then were there two thieves crucified with him, one on the right hand, and another on the left."

Another way Pilate dishonored Christ was to crucify Him between a couple of "malefactors" (Luke 23:33), which means "evil doers" or "criminals." The Greek word in Matthew 27:38 is *lēstai*. There are two words in the Greek language for stealing. *Kleptai* is the word from which we get kleptomaniac—a petty thief who is addicted to stealing. But *lēstai* refers to a bandit or a plundering robber—a man who would kill if he had to. These men were the worst of criminals. It is likely they were associates of Barabbas, who originally was intended to be crucified between them before Jesus took his place.

B. Their Contempt (v. 44)

"The thieves also, who were crucified with him, cast the same in his teeth."

The thieves heaped the same insults on Him as the Jewish leaders, who said, "If he be the king of Israel, let him now come down from the cross, and we will believe him. He trusted in God; let him [God] deliver him now, if he will have him; for he said, I am the Son of God" (Matt. 27:43).

They probably knew something about Jesus because they were part of Jewish society. They may have had occasion to hear Him speak. We don't know for sure. Chances are they knew more about Him than the Roman legionnaires, who for the most part didn't care what happened in that part of the world.

The two thieves were wicked. They heaped insults at Jesus. The ignorant pagans were not the only ones who rejected Jesus Christ and took pleasure at his execution. For these crass, materialistic bandits, life revolved around the loot they could steal. They had no thoughts about righteousness, truth, justice, honor, and godliness. They had no concern for morality and messiahs.

There are people like that in our world today. They know about Jesus—they may not know much, but they know a little. However, for them life revolves around material things. They have little regard for righteousness or truth. They live to indulge themselves, and they pay a great price for it. The two thieves were so committed to their life-style that they continued to fire insults at the Son of God while facing their own death. They represent blasphemers who have a greater love for the things of the world than they do for the things of God.

III. THE FICKLE WICKED—THE CARELESS CROWD (vv. 39-40)

The careless crowd represents people who hear Christ's words and invite Him to be a part of their life but eventually turn away.

A. Their Decreasing Enthusiasm (v. 39a)

"And they that passed by."

We can be sure many people passed by Jesus since victims were crucified along a highway. The crucifixion took place directly outside the wall of Jerusalem along a road heading north. It was frequently traveled, and especially this day since it was the Passover. Pilgrims swelled the city as many prepared to eat the Passover that evening. With so much traffic, the scene of the crucifixion was a busy place.

The same crowd that cried, "Crucify Him!" had hailed Him a few days earlier with their hosannas (Matt. 21:10). They hailed Him as their Messiah, the Savior, the one who would deliver them from Rome's oppression. But they were fickle. They had a place for Jesus: they wanted to see His miracles, signs, and wonders. They were awed by His teaching and His confrontation of the evil religious leaders. Jesus fascinated them. They knew who He claimed to be and had seen Him demonstrate the veracity of those claims. But now He was a victim of the Romans, so they rejected Him.

B. Their Increasing Rejection (vv. 39b-40)

1. Physical taunting (v. 39b)

"[They] reviled Him, wagging their heads."

The Greek word translated "reviled" is in the imperfect tense, which indicates that they kept on reviling Him with continual defamation and blasphemy. They wagged their heads in taunting fashion. Psalm 22:7-8 predicted that would happen: "All they who see me laugh me to scorn; they shoot out the lip, they shake the head, saying, He trusted on the Lord that he would deliver him; let him deliver him." They weren't trying to fulfill Scripture; they didn't even consider it.

2. Verbal taunting (v. 40)

"And saying, Thou that destroyest the temple, and buildest it in three days, save thyself. If thou be the Son of God, come down from the cross."

a) The claims

Why did they say that? Because those were the two accusations that came out against Christ in the trial before Annas and Caiaphas.

(1) He would raise the Temple

The religious leaders had gathered false witnesses who said, "This fellow [Jesus] said, I am able to destroy the temple of God, and to build it in three days" (Matt. 26:61). They tried to come up with a crime because they wanted to kill Jesus. The Jewish leaders knew what the verdict was going to be; they just didn't have a crime to fit it. So they bribed false witnesses to give false testimony. Jesus did say, "Destroy this temple, and in three days I will raise it up" (John 2:19), but He was referring to the temple of His body (v. 21). So the leaders perverted one of Jesus' statements to use against Him, claiming He was intending to destroy their Temple.

(2) He claimed to be the Son of God

In Matthew 26:63-64 Caiaphas says to Jesus, "I adjure thee by the living God, that thou tell us whether thou be the Christ, the Son of God. Jesus saith unto him, Thou hast said" (cf. Mark 14:61-62*a*). He was condemned for clearly stating the truth.

b) The challenge

The leaders now used the same accusations to incite the passers-by to mock Christ as He suffered on the cross. The people obliged, saying, "So You're going to destroy the Temple and then build it in three days? Well, let's see You show Your power by getting off that cross—some Son of God!" It wasn't enough for Christ to die; they had to taunt Him in the process. The mindless, fickle crowd that was throwing palm branches at His feet and hailing Him as the Messiah on Monday was now mocking and blaspheming His name on Friday.

c) The conviction

Jesus didn't fulfill the crowd's expectation. When He rode into Jerusalem on Monday, they thought He would attack the Romans. But He didn't. For an entire week He had done nothing, and now He was hanging on a cross, put there by the Romans. They thought He couldn't be their Messiah because He had become a victim.

The affirmation from Pilate that Jesus was innocent added to their conviction that Jesus wasn't their Messiah. They assumed the Messiah would lead them in military triumph over Rome and all the other nations. The crowd had forgotten their hallelujahs and hosannas in their disappointment over Jesus' failure to give them what they wanted when they wanted it. So they turned against Him and blasphemed His name.

The fickle crowd is reminiscent of evil people today. Many people have been to church: perhaps they were reared in the church and know the message of salvation. Maybe they've had Christian training and made a profession of faith at some point. But that was all in the past, and they are no longer interested. Since then they've gone on to other things. They're interested in Jesus only if He can bring immediate satisfaction—if He doesn't deliver what they want when they want it, they forget Him. I grieve about that. The person who knows about the claims and power of Jesus has a great responsibility to respond to that knowledge. If he walks away, he will receive the severer punishment.

The mother of a young man approached me on one occasion and said, "I raised my son in the church and in the things of the Lord, but now he's decided to be a homosexual." What a tragedy! He represents the fickle crowd that finds something they want more than Jesus Christ. At one time they sing the songs and hail Him; at another time they blaspheme His name. The world is full of people who at one time hailed Jesus but now taunt Him. They never had salvation. They knew the truth about Jesus but rejected it. The fickle wicked are traitors.

IV. THE RELIGIOUS WICKED—THE CRUEL LEADERS (vv. 41-43)

A. The Hypocritical Authorities (v. 41)

"Likewise also the chief priests, mocking him, with the scribes and elders."

The religious leaders were insincere and hypocritical. They were the lowest level of blasphemers—religious hypocrites who paraded their supposed piety. They appeared to represent God, to know the truth, and to be pure, godly, and virtuous—but they hated Christ.

The chief priests were the upper level of priests who served in the Temple ministries. The scribes were the authorities on the law. And the elders were supposed to be the revered men of wisdom and maturity in the land. Those three groups constituted the Sanhedrin—the ruling body of Israel. The religious elite—who supposedly knew everything there was to know about God—mocked Jesus. Notice that they didn't talk to Christ in the way the crowd did. They despised Him so much that they wouldn't talk to Him, so they talked to each other about Him.

B. The Hateful Attacks (vv. 42-43)

1. Against Christ's Power (v. 42)

    a) His healing ministry (v. 42*a*)

    "He saved others; himself He cannot save."

    The leaders were referring to Jesus' deliverance of people from demons. The leaders never once denied the miracles of Jesus. It was impossible to do that. To get around the obvious problem, they attributed them to Satan's power (Matt. 12:24). When Jesus did not come down from the cross, they were sure of it. They believed God was on their side, and that His greater power kept Christ on the cross.

    b) His sovereignty (v. 42*b*)

    "If he be the King of Israel, let him now come down from the cross, and we will believe him."

    They wanted to see His power and sovereignty in action right then. They had often asked for a sign (e.g., Matt. 12:38-41). Yet even if He had come down from the cross, they wouldn't have believed Him. That's how evil their hearts were. They were not sincere in their request; they were mocking and laughing at Him. They had no idea why Christ would remain on the cross if He really had the power to come down. They didn't understand the concept of a sacrificial death.

2. Against Christ's person (v. 43)

    "He trusted in God; let him deliver him now, if he will have him; for he said, I am the Son of God."

That verse is the fulfillment of Psalm 22:8. The truthfulness of the prophetic Word was declared at the cross.

Jesus claimed to be the Son of God on many occasions—most recently in response to Caiaphas's question (Matt. 26:63). The religious wicked had nothing to do with God. They were blind leaders, apostates, false teachers, hypocrites, and wolves in sheep's clothing, doomed to hell.

Conclusion

Every unbeliever fits into one of four categories: he is either an ignorant unbeliever, a knowledgeable unbeliever, a fickle unbeliever, or a religious unbeliever.

A. The Guilty

Every unbeliever, no matter when he lives, is as guilty as the unbelievers who witnessed the crucifixion of Christ.

1. Zechariah 12:10—Someday Israel will look on Him "whom they have pierced, and they shall mourn for him, as one mourneth for his only son." The people who will be alive at the time Zechariah is referring to will be just as guilty as those who put Christ on the cross.

2. Hebrews 6:6—Those who reject Christ "crucify to themselves the Son of God afresh, and put him to an open shame." You either stand with the believers or the crucifiers.

B. The Forgiven

What sticks in my mind regarding the crucifixion of Christ is His saying, "Father, forgive them; for they know not what they do" (Luke 23:34). Jesus Christ, the friend of sinners, would not come down from the cross because He had to die for the ignorant soldiers, the knowing thieves, the fickle crowd, and the vile religious leaders. So great is the compassion of God that Christ died for all who would crucify Him.

1. A centurion

   Matthew 27:54 says, "When the centurion, and they that were with him watching [guarding] Jesus." Who was he? Verse 36 tells us that the Roman soldiers put Him on the cross and then sat down and watched Him. This centurion was the leader of those men. Verse 54 continues, "[When they] saw the earthquake, and those things that were done, they feared greatly, saying, Truly, this was the Son of God." Luke 23:47 says, "When the centurion saw what was done, he glorified God, saying, Certainly this was a righteous man." I believe Scripture indicates the centurion came to embrace Jesus Christ as Savior that day. By the saving grace of God, he and perhaps some of his companions were plucked out of the group of the ignorant wicked to embrace the Savior they crucified.

2. A thief

   Luke 23:39-43 says, "One of the malefactors who were hanged railed at him [Jesus], saying, If thou be the Christ, save thyself and us. But the other, answering, rebuked him, saying, Dost not thou fear God, seeing thou art in the same condemnation? And we, indeed, justly; for we receive the due reward of our deeds. But this man hath done nothing amiss. And he said unto Jesus, Lord, remember me when thou comest into thy kingdom. And Jesus said unto him, Verily I say unto thee, Today shalt thou be with me in paradise." Here are the knowing wicked—one self-indulgent thief heaping insults of blasphemy on Jesus Christ and the other crying out for mercy to the only one who can save him.

3. A crowd

   The apostle Peter, on the Day of Pentecost, launched into a great sermon about Christ (Acts 2:14-40). He indicts the Jews for the crucifixion of Christ in verse 23. In verse 24 he talks about the resurrection of the Lord. Then in verse 36 he says, "God hath made that same Jesus, whom ye have crucified, both Lord and Christ." What happened? The people "were pricked in their heart, and said unto Peter and to the rest of the apostles, Men and brethren, what shall we do? Then Peter said unto them, Repent, and be baptized, every one of you, in the name of Jesus Christ for the remission of sins, and ye shall receive the gift of the Holy Spirit. . . . They that gladly received his word were baptized; and the same day there were added unto them about three thousand souls" (vv. 37-38, 41). God, in His sovereign grace, saved three thousand souls out of the crowd that rejected Christ, screamed for His crucifixion, and reviled Him on the cross. Verse 47 says more were added every day.

4. A company of priests

The church was beginning to flourish as more people were led to the Savior. Acts 6:7 says, "The word of God increased, and the number of the disciples multiplied in Jerusalem greatly; and a great company of the priests were obedient to the faith." I'm confident that God saved some of the religious leaders who mocked and blasphemed the name of Jesus Christ.

Jesus is indeed the friend of sinners. He died on the cross to bear the sins of the very ones who crucified Him—and those of all ages who reject Him. He calls sinners to Himself out of each group. He is able and eager to forgive. Where are you? If you're in one of those groups of rejecters, know that Christ died for you. He longs to embrace you and give you the salvation He so freely provided. He stayed on the cross not because He couldn't come down, but because He wouldn't come down. The Savior shed tears for those who shed His blood. Such is the compassion of God and the gift of salvation.

Focusing on the Facts

1. In what ways did Jesus experience sorrow (see p. 69)?
2. How did Jesus Christ suffer (see pp. 69-70)?
3. Whose blood will be on Christ's robe when He returns in glory? What kind of crown will He wear? What kind of scepter will He wield (Rev. 19:12-15; see p. 71)?
4. Describe how a person was crucified (see pp. 71-72).

5. What kind of thieves were crucified on either side of Jesus (see p. 73)?
6. Why can we probably conclude that the thieves knew about Christ (see p. 73)?
7. Why did so many people pass by the scene of Christ's crucifixion (see p. 74)?
8. Why did the crowd taunt Jesus the way they did (Matt. 27:40; see pp. 75-76)?
9. Why didn't the Jewish crowd believe Jesus was their Messiah (see p. 76)?
10. Who were the chief priests, scribes, and elders (see p. 77)?
11. What aspects of Christ's work did the religious leaders mock (Matt. 27:42-43; see pp. 78-79)?
12. Give examples of people who were forgiven, even though they either mocked or crucified Jesus (see pp. 79-81).

Pondering the Principles

1. Review the section on the sufferings of Christ (see pp. 69-70). If rated on a scale of 1-10, Christ's sufferings are a 10. How do your own sufferings rate? To what degree do you share in the sufferings of Christ? Read 1 Peter 4:1-2, 12-19. The apostle Peter learned some valuable lessons from our Lord about suffering. What one lesson can you apply to your life today?

2. Review the conclusion of this lesson (see pp. 79-81). You might know of some unbelievers who fit into one of the four categories of the wicked. How do you perceive them? Do you resent them because they reject Jesus Christ? Or do you resent them because they reject what you believe about Christ? What was Christ's attitude toward all the wicked people who mocked Him (Luke 23:34)? How might you apply Christ's attitude to the relationships you have established with unbelievers?

5
God's Miraculous Commentary on the Cross

Outline

Introduction
A. The Meaning of the Cross in the Old Testament
B. The Meaning of the Cross in the New Testament

Lesson
I. Supernatural Darkness (v. 45)
   A. The Time of the Darkness
   B. The Extent of the Darkness
     1. The examples
       a) Exodus 10:22-23
       b) Joshua 10:12-14
       c) 2 Kings 20:9-11
     2. The explanation
   C. The Meaning of the Darkness
     1. The traditional views
     2. The biblical view
       a) Isaiah 5:26-30
       b) Isaiah 13:10-11
       c) Matthew 24:29-30
II. Sovereign Departure (vv. 46-49)
   A. The Cry of Christ (v. 46)
     1. The explanation of the separation
       a) The testimony of the Father
       b) The testimony of Scripture
     2. The essence of the separation
       a) At the incarnation
       b) At the cross
         (1) Christ's hatred of sin
         (2) Christ's longing for God

Introduction

Most people are aware of the death of Jesus Christ, but they have little understanding of its significance. Each year at Easter, many people hear about the crucifixion and resurrection. What do the death and resurrection of Christ mean? History tells us that 30,000 Jews were crucified by the Romans around the time of Jesus Christ. Why do we remember only one of them? Even the two thieves who died on either side of Christ remain nameless. Surely others died because they were uncompromising in something they stood for. Certainly others were examples of love, character, honesty, and integrity. So why does history celebrate only the death of Jesus Christ? In what way is it significant? The answer is in the Word of God.

A. The Meaning of the Cross in the Old Testament

Genesis 3:15 promised the coming of One called the "seed of the woman." But it's the man, not the woman, who has seed. The title refers to a virgin birth. Verse 15 says the One born of the woman would bruise the serpent's head, even though He would be bruised in the heel. While Christ was being bruised on the cross, He was fatally bruising the one who was bruising Him—the devil.

We learn more about the meaning of the cross through the lives of Abraham and Isaac. God called Abraham to offer his son on the altar as a sacrifice (Gen. 22:2). As he was ready to kill his son, Abraham discovered that God provided an alternative—a ram caught in the thicket (22:12-13). Here we learn about the provision of a substitute for one who ought to die.

The Mosaic law, and all the ceremonies and sacrifices accompanying it, delineate the need for a blood sacrifice to atone for sin. Other passages in the Old Testament fill in other details about the cross (e.g., Ps. 22, Isa. 53, Zech. 12).

B. The Meaning of the Cross in the New Testament

The apostle Paul tells us that God made Christ a curse for us when He was put on the cross (Gal. 3:13). The apostle Peter says He who was just suffered the sins of the unjust (1 Pet. 3:18). The apostle John describes Jesus as a lamb slain (Rev. 5:9). The writer of Hebrews tells us Christ was offered once for the sins of the world (Heb. 10:10).

If we want to know the meaning of the cross, we have only to look from beginning to end in holy Scripture. However, I believe one monumental description of the meaning of the cross is often overlooked: the one given in Matthew 27:45-53.

Six miracles attended the death of Jesus Christ. They are God's commentary on the meaning of the cross.

Lesson

I. SUPERNATURAL DARKNESS (v. 45)

"Now from the sixth hour there was darkness over all the land unto the ninth hour."

Luke 2:9-11 tells us that when Christ was born, a great light appeared in the sky. The prophet Isaiah said the Messiah would be a light to the Gentiles (Isa. 49:6). Of Himself Jesus said, "I am the light of the world; he that followeth me shall not walk in darkness" (John 8:12). He also said, "While ye have light, believe in the light" (John 12:36). Associated with the birth, life, and ministry of Christ is light. But associated with His death is darkness.

A. The Time of the Darkness

From the sixth hour (12:00 noon) to the ninth hour (3:00 P.M.), the sun became dark. That is the time of day when the sun is at its zenith. Mark 15:25 tells us Jesus was crucified at the third hour (9:00 A.M.). Jesus had been on the cross for three hours by the time it became dark. He remained there another three hours before He died at the ninth hour (3:00 P.M.).

Jesus Breaks His Silence

Jesus broke His silence only three times during the first three hours He hung on the cross.

1. To offer forgiveness

The first time He said, "Father, forgive them; for they know not what they do" (Luke 23:34). He said that on behalf of the Roman soldiers who crucified Him.

2. To save a thief

Later, He broke the silence again by saying this to the repentant thief hanging beside Him, "Verily I say unto thee, Today shalt thou be with me in paradise" (Luke 23:43).

3. To care for His mother

He broke silence a third time when He saw the apostle John and His mother, Mary, standing at the foot of the cross. Knowing they would be lost without Him, He committed them to each other (John 19:26-27).

Apart from those three occasions, the three hours from nine to noon were unbroken by any word from Christ.

B. The Extent of the Darkness

As the second three hours began, the land became dark instantaneously. The Greek word translated "land" is *gē*. It could also be translated as "earth." We don't know if the darkness engulfed the land of Israel only, Jerusalem and its environs, or the half of the earth normally engulfed in sunlight. God could do any of those things.

1. The examples

   a) Exodus 10:22-23—God made it dark in the land of Egypt only. He can create localized darkness if He desires.

   b) Joshua 10:12-14—Here the Lord made the sun stand still—it stayed in one spot in the sky. That means the earth had to stop revolving for a period of time while God did His work. What an impact that must have made on the world!

   c) 2 Kings 20:9-11—The shadow on a sundial went backwards as a sign to King Hezekiah that he would recover from his illness. God again performed a miracle with the earth's revolution.

   There are some indications from extrabiblical literature that the half of the earth in daylight became dark. Third-century church Father Origen referred to a statement by the Roman historian Phlegon, who mentioned that unusual darkness (*Against Celsus* II.33). Tertullian, when referring to the darkness to his pagan audience, said,

"You yourselves have the account of the world-portent still in your archives" (*Apology* XXI).

2. The explanation

Some have suggested that maybe a cloud passed in front of the sun or that maybe it was a sirocco (an east wind that accumulates dust to such a degree that the sky appears black). However, it could not have been either of those because Luke 23:45 clearly says, "The sun was darkened." Luke used the Greek word *ekleipō*, from which we get the word *eclipse*. It literally means "to fail utterly." The sun failed—God darkened it supernaturally. Now if in so doing God allowed the normal sequence of events to take place, the world would have gone out of existence. Somehow God turned out the sun and sustained the world.

The darkness was not technically an eclipse. The sun and the moon are at opposite ends of the earth at the time of year when the Passover is celebrated. An eclipse can occur only when they're in the same location in the sky. Since this was not a scientific eclipse, we can take *ekleipō* in its broad meaning: "the sun failed." The land became as dark as midnight in the middle of the day.

C. The Meaning of the Darkness

1. The traditional views

The rabbis taught that the sun's failing indicates God's judgment on the world for committing a great crime. Certainly the world committed a great crime in crucifying Jesus Christ. Others suggest the sun went dark because nature dropped a veil over the sufferings of Christ. Some believe the darkness was a sympathetic act on God's part to cover the nakedness and dishonor of His Son. Others think the darkness was a divine protest.

2. The biblical view

What is the true meaning of the darkness? What was God saying? Not one biblical writer comments on the darkness at the cross of Christ. They didn't need to, because the Old Testament clearly states what it means. Darkness was a symbol of divine judgment.

a) Isaiah 5:26-30—Isaiah predicted the coming judgment of Israel, when its life would be choked out and its people taken into captivity. He described it as a time of darkness and sorrow.

b) Isaiah 13:10-11—Here Isaiah looks ahead to God's final judgment on the world. He says, "The stars of heaven and the constellations thereof shall not give their light; the sun shall be darkened in its going forth, and the moon shall not cause its light to shine. And I will punish the world for its evil, and the wicked for their iniquity." God associates darkness with judgment.

c) Matthew 24:29-30—"Immediately after the tribulation of those days shall the sun be darkened, and the moon shall not give its light, and the stars shall fall from heaven, and the powers of the heavens shall be shaken. And then shall appear the sign of the Son of man in heaven." Man will be horrified at the unrelenting darkness God will bring to the world.

Throughout Scripture you will find judgment associated with darkness (e.g., Joel 2:30-31; Amos 5:18, 20; Zeph. 1:14-18). If God's salvation is seen as light, His judgment is seen as darkness. Both the Old Testament and New Testament writers refer to it. When rebellious angels were cast out of heaven, they were bound in chains of darkness (2 Pet. 2:4).

The darkness at the crucifixion of Christ represents God's divine judgment. The cross became the place for the pouring out of His wrath. Jesus Christ was not just one man among 30,000 people who were crucified. He was not some well-meaning martyr. He was the recipient of divine judgment. There is only one thing that God judges, and that's sin. The darkness at the cross was the Father's commentary on His judgment of sin. The crucifixion of Christ was much bigger than one man's dying for something He believed in.

II. SOVEREIGN DEPARTURE (vv. 46-49)

A. The Cry of Christ (v. 46)

"About the ninth hour [3:00 P.M.] Jesus cried with a loud voice, saying, Eli, Eli [Hebrew], lama sabachthani [Aramaic]? that is to say, My God, my God, why hast thou forsaken me?"

The people knew Jesus was quoting Psalm 22:1. The Jews knew it well because they had no doubt chanted it, recited it, and memorized it. Even those Jews who spoke predominantly Aramaic and knew little Hebrew knew *Eli* referred to God because *El* was the name for God.

This was a miracle in reverse—a supernatural event beyond human understanding—for God was separated from God. God the Father turned His back on God the Son. Tradition says Martin Luther went into seclusion to try to understand this mystery but came out more confused than when he began. I can understand that. After experiencing the fury of God, Jesus cried out as He was separated from the Father.

1. The explanation of the separation

Why was Jesus separated from God?

a) The testimony of the Father

Habakkuk 1:13 says this about God: "Thou art of purer eyes than to behold evil, and canst not look on iniquity." God turned His back on Jesus because He can't look on sin. What does that tell us about the cross? That Jesus actually became sin for us (2 Cor. 5:21). If this was the death of a loving martyr, of an innocent person who had a good cause, God would have looked on Him with favor. But when He turned His back on Jesus, He was confirming that Christ was bearing our sin.

b) The testimony of Scripture

Isaiah 53:5 says, "He was wounded for our transgressions." Romans 4:25 says He was "delivered for our offenses." First Corinthians 15:3 says, "Christ died for our sins." First Peter 2:24 says Christ "bore our sins in his own body on the tree." First Peter 3:18 says, "Christ also hath once suffered for sins, the just for the unjust." First John 4:10 says God "sent his Son to be the propitiation [atonement] for our sins." Galatians 3:13 says Christ was "made a curse for us." And 2 Corinthians 5:21 says God "made him, who knew no sin, to be sin for us."

Christ didn't just bear sin; He *became* sin. He bore all the sins of all people of all ages. Thus Hebrews 2:9 says He "tasted death for every man." That's why He came to earth. Matthew 20:28 says, "The Son of man came not to be ministered unto, but to minister, and to give his life a ransom for many." God forsook Christ because He cannot look on sin.

2. The essence of the separation

What kind of separation did Jesus experience? He wasn't separated from His divine nature—He didn't cease to be God, or He would have ceased to exist. He was not separated from the Trinity in essence or substance, but He was separated in terms of intimate fellowship and communion. When a child sins against his father, he does not cease to be his father's child. However, he does cease to know the intimacy of loving communion with him on account of the sin. In the same way God had to turn His back on Christ.

a) At the incarnation

When Christ first came into the world, He experienced a certain separation from God. Philippians 2:6-7 says Jesus "did not regard equality with God a thing to be grasped, but emptied Himself, taking the form of a bond servant" (NASB*). When Christ became incarnate, He let go of some of His equality with God. Jesus asked His Father to restore the glory He had with Him before the world began (John 17:5).

b) At the cross

On the cross Jesus experienced an even more profound separation—the separation of utter sinfulness. When God turned His back on Jesus Christ, He was turning from sin and not from Christ. God will always turn His back on sin.

(1) Christ's hatred of sin

Jesus bore the weight of all the sin of all the ages, yet He Himself was never a sinner. In the midst of being engulfed in all that sin, He never had a desire for it. He hated it.

(2) Christ's longing for God

Jesus expressed His longing in these words: "My God, my God, why hast thou forsaken me?" What did Jesus long for? God. Therein lies the evidence of His pure spirit—a purity He maintained. Soon after that He said, "It is finished" (John 19:30). Then He said, "Father, into thy hands I commend my spirit" (Luke 23:46). Jesus said that, knowing full well God would accept Him. Even though He bore sin, He never became a sinner. That is why the writer of Hebrews said He is "yet without sin" (Heb. 4:15). He was made sin, but He did not sin—that is a great paradox of the Christian faith.

The second miracle that occurred on the cross was the Father's turning His back on the Son. What does that teach us? That Christ became sin as He bore the sins of man.

*New American Standard Bible.

B. The Mockery of the Crowd (vv. 47-49)

1. Taunting rejection (v. 47)

"Some of them that stood there, when they heard that, said, This man calleth for Elijah."

They knew He didn't say, "Elias, Elias." They knew He was saying, "Eli, Eli"—"My God, my God." They were mocking Him again. The prophet Malachi said that before Messiah came to set up His kingdom Elijah would come (Mal. 4:5). They were saying, "This poor, misguided Messiah still thinks He's going to have His kingdom. Maybe He's calling for Elijah to announce Him as Messiah and proclaim His kingdom!" Their mockery was cruel, cynical, and sarcastic.

2. Temporary relief (v. 48)

"Straightway one of them [probably a Roman soldier] ran, and took a sponge, and filled it with vinegar, and put it on a reed, and gave him to drink."

John 19:28 tells us Jesus said, "I thirst," which led to what happened in Matthew 27:48. Great thirst certainly was part of the torture of crucifixion. John 19:29 says the sponge was put on a hyssop reed, which measured about eighteen inches. That indicates the cross stood low to the ground. The sponge was lifted up to Jesus' lips so He might moisten them to help quench His thirst. The King James Version says Jesus was given vinegar. The Greek word is *oxos*, which was a cheap, sour wine containing a high percentage of water and a low percentage of alcohol. It was a common drink that laborers and soldiers used to quench their thirst.

When His torturers gave Christ the wine, was that an act of mercy? It may have been, but it only served to prolong His agony.

3. Thoughtless reckoning (v. 49)

"The rest said, Let be; let us see whether Elijah will come to save him."

The crowd saw the thirst of Christ as just one more thing to mock. They carried out their malicious mockery as far as they could, until He finally died.

The people missed God's purpose in the crucifixion of Christ. It's hard to imagine, but they mocked Christ during the darkness that covered the land. You would think they would have considered that darkness more carefully. They should have remembered Isaiah's words about darkness and judgment. They should have remembered that other prophets associated darkness with judgment. They could have realized that Joel's prediction was coming to pass (Joel 2:31). When they heard Jesus cry, "My God, my God, why hast thou forsaken me?" they might have understood He was bearing their sin. But that meant they had to understand God requires a perfect sacrifice for sin. They didn't realize that sacrifice was Christ. So they ignored the darkness and mocked Jesus.

III. SACRIFICIAL DEATH (v. 50)

"Jesus, when He had cried again with a loud voice, yielded up the spirit."

A. The Verbal Demonstration of Christ's Strength

Jesus had broken His silence five times previously. The first three occurred in the first three hours. Then in the hours of darkness He said, "My God, my God, why hast thou forsaken me?" and, "I thirst." Now just before He yielded up His life, He cried with a loud voice. It's important that His cries in the last three hours of His life were with a "loud voice," because they demonstrate that He still possessed physical strength. He had not reached utter exhaustion. That made clear that He had the resources to stay alive. John 19:30 says He cried, "It is finished." Then He cried, "Father, into thy hands I commend my spirit" (Luke 23:46).

B. The Voluntary Nature of Christ's Death

After crying out, Jesus "gave up the spirit" (Luke 23:46). Other places in Scripture that refer to someone's giving up the spirit use a Greek word that speaks of one breathing his last. However, Matthew and John didn't use that word in describing the death of Jesus. They used two words that refer to someone who is handing over his life of his own accord. Jesus sent His spirit away as an act of His will. Here lies the third miracle of the cross: Jesus' life was not taken from Him; He voluntarily gave it up.

1. Its demonstration

   Christ's voluntary death is demonstrated in its speed. Victims normally lingered for days on the cross, but Christ died after six hours. According to Mark 15:44-45, Pilate was astonished when he heard Jesus was dead. He even sent someone to check, because it was so unusual for anyone to die that soon.

2. Its power

   Jesus had the power not only to take His life out of the grave but also to give it up whenever He wished. No man has the power to do that any more than he has the power to raise himself. You could shoot yourself, but that means you give yourself up to the bullet. You could take poison, but that means you give yourself up to the poison. You could throw yourself off a bridge, but that means you give yourself up to the fall. Jesus has power over death and life. No one took His life from Him; He freely gave it.

   John 10:11 says, "I am the good shepherd; the good shepherd giveth his life for the sheep." Verse 15 says, "I lay down my life for the sheep." Verses 17-18 say, "I lay down my life, that I might take it again. No man taketh it from me, but I lay it down of myself. I have power to lay it down, and I have power to take it again." The cross reveals that only God, who controls both death and life, could voluntarily sacrifice Himself.

IV. SYMBOLIC DEVASTATION (v. 51*a*)

   "Behold, the veil of the temple was torn in two from the top to the bottom."

A. Limited Access to the Temple

1. The symbol of God's presence with man

    The word *temple* does not refer to the whole Temple; it is translated from the Greek word *naos*, which here refers to the inner sanctuary—the Holy of Holies. That was the dwelling place of His symbolic presence. A great curtain covered the Holy of Holies. No one could enter it except the high priest once a year on the Day of Atonement. On that day he sprinkled blood on the altar for the sins of the people.

2. The symbol of God's separation from man

    That only the priest could enter the Holy of Holies symbolized that no man had true access to the presence of God. None of the sacrifices actually atoned for sin; they were symbols. No lamb, goat, ram, turtledove, or pigeon was ever sufficient to atone for sin because no one could keep the law of God. No man's righteousness was adequate to allow him access to God. That fact was continually before the people because God's dwelling place was veiled from them—they couldn't enter the Holy of Holies. God cannot receive sinners into His presence until their sin is dealt with. The curtain kept men from God in the sense of true intimacy. It symbolized man's separation from God.

B. Unlimited Access to God

When Christ died, the veil was ripped from top to bottom. At that moment, the Temple would have been filled with pilgrims and priests performing sacrifices. Suddenly, to anyone ministering in the Holy Place, the Holy of Holies was exposed.

1. The beginning of internal worship

    In the death of Jesus Christ, God was saying that there is now total access to His holy presence. Why? Because Christ paid the penalty for sin. God throws His arms wide open to sinners. As a result, the writer of Hebrews could say, "Let us, therefore, come boldly unto the throne of grace, that we may obtain mercy, and find grace to help in time of need" (Heb. 4:16). We now can rush into the presence of God. The separation no longer exists because the death of Jesus Christ removed it. The barrier is no more.

2. The end of external sacrifices

When God ripped the curtain to the Holy of Holies, He pronounced the end of the Judaistic system. It was the end of the sacrifices and the priesthood. Within a few years, the Gentiles desecrated and trampled the Temple into oblivion. That destruction began when God ripped the veil.

When Christ died, access to God became a reality. The Old Covenant was over. God initiated a New Covenant through the blood of Christ. He made His holy presence available to all who would come in the name of Christ to have their sins forgiven. Notice that the curtain was ripped from the top to the bottom. That shows us men didn't do it: it was a supernatural act of God. God opened His presence to everyone who comes in the name of Jesus Christ.

V. SUDDEN DESTRUCTION (v. 51*b*)

"The earth did quake, and the rocks were split."

At the death of Jesus Christ, the Father brought about a devastating earthquake in Jerusalem that split open rocks and created fissures in the ground.

A. A Sign of God's Appearance

In the Old Testament, earthquakes frequently preceded God's appearance (Ex. 19:18; 1 Kings 19:11; 2 Sam. 22:8; Pss. 18:7; 77:18; Isa. 29:6; Jer. 10:10; Nah. 1:2, 5).

B. A Sign of God's Judgment

Someday the world and the heavens are going to shake to the point of destruction. Revelation 6:12-13 tells us that the stars will fall, the constellations will come apart, and the light of the sun and the moon will go out.

1. A work of regeneration

There will be a great shaking of the earth in the final judgment. Why? Because God is going to redo this cursed earth. In the original creation there were no earthquakes. God created a perfect environment for Adam and his race. Man was to enjoy the presence of God in the perfection He intended for paradise. But when Adam sinned, not only he and his wife were cursed, but the earth was cursed as well. To this day the earth is rocking and reeling under that curse. Romans 8:22 says all creation groans, waiting for its return to what Milton entitled his famous epic: *Paradise Regained.* The Bible promises a new heaven and a new earth. Someday the earth will be what it is supposed to be. Someday the usurper, Satan, will be deposed from his rule. Christ will become the new monarch. The earth will no longer be cursed; it will be a glorious new earth.

Hebrews 12:26-28 says, "Yet once more I [the Lord] shake not the earth only, but also heaven. And this word, Yet once more, signifieth the removing of those things that are shaken, as of things that are made, that those things which cannot be shaken may remain. Wherefore, receiving a kingdom which cannot be moved." God is going to shake the old earth out of existence and make a brand new one—a new earth and new heaven in which Christ will reign supreme as King of kings and Lord of lords.

2. A work of redemption

What does the future of the earth have to do with what happened at the cross? When God shook the earth at the death of Christ, I think He was giving the world a taste of what will happen in the future when the King returns. When Jesus died on the cross, He so perfectly accomplished the Father's will that He earned the right to be King of the earth. He earned the right to take the title deed to the earth out of the hand of God (Rev. 5:7). One day He will unroll that deed and begin the process of taking over the earth (Rev. 6-19). When Christ finished the work of redemption, the Father said, "Sit thou at my right hand until I make thine enemies thy footstool." Philippians 2:10 says, "At the name of Jesus every knee should bow, of things in heaven, and things in earth, and things under the earth." The shaking of the earth at the death of Christ was God's way of guaranteeing the promise of a renewed world and universe.

VI. SUBSEQUENT DELIVERANCE (vv. 52-53)

A. The Resurrection of the Saints (vv. 52-53a)

"The graves were opened; and many bodies [Gk., *somata*] of the saints that slept were raised, and came out of the graves."

This was a real resurrection of bodies, not just spirits. Not all bodies were raised, only select Old Testament saints. When Jesus died, their spirits came from the dwelling place of righteous spirits. They were joined with their glorified bodies, which came out of those graves.

B. The Testimony of the Saints (v. 53b)

"After his [Christ's] resurrection, [they] went into the holy city, and appeared unto many."

You can imagine the kind of testimony they had about Christ's resurrection. Why didn't they go into the city to testify until after Christ rose? Because 1 Corinthians 15:20 says, "Now Christ is risen from the dead and become the first fruits of them that slept." So they didn't begin to speak until after Christ rose from the dead.

I don't believe they spoke to anyone except those who already believed. There's no biblical evidence of Christ's ever appearing after His resurrection to anyone other than believers. I'm sure the believers were thrilled to meet them. The risen saints would have testified that Christ was alive, guaranteeing the reality of resurrection for all believers. They became living proof of that guarantee.

The cross is the greatest hope for resurrection because Christ paid for your sin. You are free from death and free to live. In His kingdom we will have glorified bodies like His.

Conclusion

What do we see at the cross? The wrath of God is depicted in supernatural darkness. The holiness of God is seen when He turned from Christ, who had become sin. The grace and mercy of God is depicted in Christ's voluntary act of self-sacrifice to redeem unworthy men. The curtain in the Temple is ripped from top to bottom as God opens the way of access to Himself. The shaking of the earth reminds us that the promised new earth and heaven will come. Jesus will reign as King of kings and Lord of lords, and we'll be there to reign with Him. And the resurrection of the saints at the death of Christ guarantees the resurrection of all who believe in Him. That is God's supernatural testimony of the meaning of His Son's death.

Focusing on the Facts

1. What does the Old Testament teach about the meaning of the cross (see p. 85)?
2. What does the New Testament teach about the meaning of the cross (see p. 85)?
3. What is associated with the birth, life, and ministry of Jesus Christ? What is associated with His death (see p. 86)?
4. How many times did Jesus break His silence during the first three hours of His crucifixion? What did He say (see pp. 86-87)?
5. What are some examples of occasions when God created supernatural darkness (see p. 87)?
6. What caused the darkness at the crucifixion (Luke 23:45; see p. 88)?
7. What does darkness typically symbolize in the Old Testament? Give some examples (see p. 89).
8. What did the darkness at the crucifixion mean (see p. 89)?
9. Why does Jesus cry out to God in Matthew 27:46? What did that confirm about the purpose of the cross (see p. 90)?
10. What did Christ do in addition to bearing man's sin (2 Cor. 5:21; see p. 91)?
11. Describe the essence of Christ's separation from God (see pp. 91-92).

12. In the midst of bearing the world's sin, what did Christ long for (see p. 92)?
13. What did the crowd do to Jesus in spite of the darkness in the land (Matt. 27:47, 49; see pp. 93-94)?
14. Why is it significant that Jesus cried loudly before He yielded up His spirit (see p. 94)?
15. How do we know that Christ's death was voluntary? Explain (see pp. 94-95).
16. Why was Jesus able to die of His own will (see p. 95)?
17. What happened to the veil shielding the Holy of Holies when Christ died (Matt. 27:51)? What did that signify (see pp. 95-96)?
18. Why will the earth shake in the final judgment of God (see p. 98)?
19. What does the shaking of the earth in the future have to do with the earthquake that occurred at the crucifixion of Christ (see pp. 98-99)?
20. Whom did God raise from the dead when Christ died? What did they do after the resurrection of Christ (Matt. 27:52-53; see p. 99)?

Pondering the Principles

1. Look up the seven statements Christ made while dying on the cross for you: Luke 23:34, Luke 23:43, John 19:26-27, Matthew 27:46, John 19:28, John 19:30, and Luke 23:46. What does each statement reveal about the His character? What do you learn about His commitment? Based on Christ's example, what should your attitude be in the midst of the severest of trials?

2. According to Habakkuk 1:13, God is too pure to look at sin. Christ suffered and died on the cross to remove your sin that God might be able to look at you. At the moment of salvation, every sin you commit is paid for by Christ's death on the cross. However, what must you do to maintain fellowship with Him (1 John 1:9)? Search your heart. Be faithful to remember what Christ endured for your sake every time you contemplate sin.

3. Hebrews 4:16 says all believers should come before God's throne of grace. That means we have access to God, something people in the Old Testament never enjoyed. According to Hebrews 4:16, why should you approach God's throne? In what

manner should you approach it? Perhaps you have not been taking advantage of the access you have to God. Examine yourself to see if there are any areas in your life that you fail to depend on God for. Bring them before Him now.

6
Responses to the Death of Christ

Outline

Introduction

Lesson
I. Saving Faith
   A. The Character of Christ's Crucifiers
      1. Their responsibility
      2. Their ignorance
      3. Their participation
   B. The Fear of Christ's Crucifiers
      1. The cause of their fear
      2. The context of their fear
      3. The conviction of their fear
   C. The Confession of Christ's Crucifiers
      1. They affirmed Christ's sonship
      2. They affirmed Christ's righteousness
      3. They glorified God
   D. The Redemption of Christ's Crucifiers
      1. The Father's forgiveness
      2. The Scripture's fulfillment
II. Shallow Conviction
   A. The Scene
      1. Initial conviction
      2. Eventual rejection
   B. The Sequel
      1. Confrontation
      2. Conviction
      3. Repentance

III. Sympathetic Loyalty
   A. The Importance of the Women
      1. Their love
      2. Their number
      3. Their service
      4. Their privilege
   B. The Identification of the Women
      1. Mary Magdalene
      2. Mary, the mother of James and Joses
      3. The mother of Zebedee's children
IV. Selfish Fear
   A. Denying the Power of Faith
   B. Violating the Principle of Discipleship

Introduction

Matthew 27:54-56 is a brief but rich passage: "When the centurion, and they that were with him watching Jesus, saw the earthquake, and those things that were done, they feared greatly, saying, Truly, this was the Son of God. And many women were there beholding afar off, who followed Jesus from Galilee, ministering unto him, among whom were Mary Magdalene and Mary, the mother of James and Joses, and the mother of Zebedee's children." In those verses and the parallel verses are four responses to the death of Christ—the same kind of responses we see today: saving faith, shallow conviction, sympathetic loyalty, and selfish fear. Two are responses of unbelievers and two of believers. These verses are part of a historical narrative, but they have practical application for our lives.

Lesson

I. SAVING FAITH

This is the best response any unbeliever could have. It is illustrated by the soldiers in Matthew 27:54: "When the centurion, and they that were with him guarding Jesus, saw the earthquake, and those things that were done, they feared greatly, saying, Truly, this was the Son of God."

A. The Character of Christ's Crucifiers

1. Their responsibility

The centurion is the focal point of our discussion about the response of saving faith. He commanded over 100 men—he was a man of some significance in the ranks of Roman soldiers. He and the men under his command were given the unique responsibility of guarding Jesus Christ. We can assume their assignment began at the start of the trial before Pilate early that morning. The centurion had to be aware of the issues surrounding Jesus. He was certain to have heard the accusations of the Jewish leaders. He also may have heard part of the conversation between Jesus and Pilate (John 18:33-38).

2. Their ignorance

The soldiers serving the centurion were the same men who nailed Jesus to the cross after mocking Him (see pp. 48-63). They were uninformed about Judaism. They were irreligious pagans. They didn't have anything against Jesus; they were at the cross of Christ because their commander wanted them there.

Jesus was nothing more to them than some bizarre character claiming to be king, although looking at Him indicated He was anything but a king. By the time Jesus arrived at Pilate's judgment hall early Friday morning, the Jewish leaders had concluded their mock trial. After the trial they had hit Him repeatedly in the face, leaving it disfigured. Jesus certainly didn't look the part of a king. He was dressed as a common man. Herod had his men put a robe on Him to mock His claim to be king. Furthermore, Jesus was silent—He didn't sound like a king. He didn't pontificate, pull rank, or call for His followers to rescue Him. The soldiers may have concluded He was mentally deranged because He accepted so much abuse without saying anything. When Jesus did have an opportunity to speak to Pilate, He spoke of a kingdom that was not of this world. So they concluded He was someone who had delusions of grandeur.

The soldiers were ignorant of whom they were dealing with. They served Pilate, which meant they were from Caesarea, a seaport city some sixty miles from Jerusalem. The Roman garrison for the Roman occupation of Israel was headquartered there. Since Jesus centered His ministry primarily in Galilee and Jerusalem, they may never have seen Jesus before this day.

3. Their participation

The centurion knew the Jews hated Christ. He had heard them scream "Crucify him!" The soldiers saw Pilate continually affirm the innocence of Jesus—all to no avail. They knew the Jewish leaders accused Jesus of claiming to be the Son of God and a king—that He was a threat to Rome and Judaism. But all that seemed ludicrous in view of the beaten and pathetic man now hanging on a cross. How could He be anything more than just a common criminal? To them He was a fake, a nobody.

B. The Fear of Christ's Crucifiers

1. The cause of their fear

Something happened, however, that changed what the soldiers thought about Jesus. Matthew 27:54 says, "When the centurion, and they that were with him watching Jesus, saw the earthquake, and those things that were done [present participle: "were occurring"]." When the sun instantly became dark at noon, when the earthquake split the ground and the rocks, and when the graves were opened, they knew something out of the ordinary was happening. Verse 54 says, "They feared greatly."

The Greek word translated "fear" is *phobeō*, from which we get the word *phobia*. The soldiers were overcome with terror—a state of panic causing the heart to beat rapidly and the body to sweat profusely. A person feels terrible anxiety in the midst of such terror. The same word is used in Matthew 14:27 to describe the fear the disciples experienced when they saw Jesus walking on water and when Jesus revealed His glory on the Mount of Transfiguration (Matt. 17:6-7).

2. The context of their fear

The soldiers were not afraid merely of the earthquake or the darkness. Inherent within their fear was spiritual awe—a reverential terror. They concluded that Jesus was not just another criminal or rebel.

3. The conviction of their fear

The centurion heard Jesus speak while He hung on the cross. He heard profound words that penetrated his heart. Now he had seen miraculous phenomena take place when Christ died. He knew something had gone wrong because the land convulsed in response. His fear indicated a sense of his sin. He feared he might be under the judgment of God. Although the soldiers were pagans, that possibility no doubt penetrated their hearts.

C. The Confession of Christ's Crucifiers

Their sense of guilt for having mocked and crucified Christ led the soldiers to another step. Fearing greatly, the centurion and some of his soldiers said, "Truly, this was the Son of God." Their fear indicates an awareness of their sin; their confession indicates salvation.

1. They affirmed Christ's sonship

If their fear merely was natural human fear, they would have cried for help or run away. However theirs was awe reserved only for God. Mark 15:39 says, "When the centurion, who stood facing him [Christ], saw that he so cried out, and gave up the spirit, he said, Truly this man was the Son of God." It wasn't just the phenomena; the final words of Jesus drove the truth into his heart. He uses the word *truly* to make clear he had no doubt in his mind. He wasn't saying, "Maybe He's the Son of God." I believe he was affirming the divine sonship of Jesus. Christ had just said, "Father, into thy hands I commend my spirit" (Luke 23:46). With His final words Jesus implied He was God's Son, and the centurion affirmed it in Matthew 27:54.

How did the centurion know Jesus was God's Son? By both the phenomena and the demeanor of Jesus on the cross—His gracious spirit, His silence when rebuked, and His victorious statement of completing His divine mission. Yet the only way anyone can ever know Jesus is God's Son is by the Holy Spirit. When Peter said, "Thou art the Christ, the Son of the living God," Jesus said, "Blessed art thou, Simon Barjona; for flesh and blood hath not revealed it unto thee, but my Father, who is in heaven" (Matt. 16:16-17). Peter knew Jesus was the Son of God because the Holy Spirit told him. First Corinthians 12:3 says, "No man can say that Jesus is the Lord, but by the Holy Spirit." You can't come to that conclusion on your own. What happened to the centurion and some of the soldiers was a work of the Holy Spirit. Through Christ's attitude and words on the cross, and through the supernatural phenomena, the Holy Spirit brought them to an affirmation of faith that can come only from God.

2. They affirmed Christ's righteousness

The centurion also said, "Certainly this was a righteous man" (Luke 23:47). Why did he say "certainly"? Once again he was affirming the truthfulness of his statement. Pilate said, "I am innocent of the blood of this righteous person" (Matt. 27:24). Pilate's wife said, "Have thou nothing to do with that righteous person" (Matt. 27:19).

3. They glorified God

Luke 23:47 says the centurion also glorified God.

He glorified the one true God, affirmed the righteousness of Jesus Christ, and declared Him to be the Son of God. That is saving faith. If the thief could receive a guarantee of salvation by saying simply, "Lord, remember me when

You come into Your kingdom," certainly the centurion could with his faith. There is no question in my mind that the centurion and perhaps several of his men were redeemed at the foot of the cross.

The Case of the Missing Article

Some have wanted to argue the validity of the centurion's faith based on linguistics. We find in Matthew 27:54 what is called an anarthrous construction in the Greek language—the phrase translated "the Son of God" has no definite article in the Greek text. The Greek doesn't translate in English to "the Son of the God," meaning the only God; it says *theou huios*—"Son of God." Some claim this pagan centurion was saying, "This man must be a son of a god"—that the centurion supposedly thought of Jesus as some offspring or emanation from one of the Roman deities. I don't think that's the intent of the text. Let me show you why.

1. The Jewish leaders didn't use the article

   The soldier used his title for Jesus based on the accusations of the Jewish leaders. According to Matthew 26:63, the high priest says to Jesus, "I adjure thee by the living God, that thou tell us whether thou be the Christ, the Son of God." The Jews believed in only one God, and they were accusing Jesus of claiming to be the only Son of the only God. That was blasphemous to them.

   According to John 19:4-5, Pilate brings Jesus before the crowd after scourging and mocking Him. The Jewish leaders screamed, "Crucify him, crucify him! . . . He made himself the Son of God" (vv. 6-7). John used the same Greek construction for what the leaders said that Matthew did for what the centurion said.

   When Caiaphas said to Jesus, "Tell us whether thou be the Christ, the Son of God," the article is used. However, when the same leaders accused Him in front of Pilate's court, the article is dropped. If the article is used in one place but not in another, yet they refer to the same thing, we can conclude that both statements refer to the same thing. In either case the leaders accused Jesus of a blasphemous claim to be the Son of God.

2. The disciples didn't use the article

Theou huios was used by the disciples in Matthew 14:33. They said, "Of a truth, thou art the Son of God." We know they didn't mean, "Truly, you are a son of a god."

3. Jesus didn't use the article

The same two words were ascribed to Jesus in Matthew 27:43.

4. Gabriel didn't use the article

The angel Gabriel told Mary that her Son would be called "the Son of God [*huios theou*]" (Luke 1:35).

The absence of an article doesn't mean you can translate the phrase, "a son of a god." The pagan centurion glorified God, affirmed Jesus as a righteous man, and called Him the Son of God. The Holy Spirit did a work in his heart, bringing him to believe in the Lord Jesus Christ. I am in agreement with Lutheran commentator Lenski, who said, "This Gentile, called Longinus in tradition, comes to faith beneath the dead Savior's cross" (*The Interpretation of St. Matthew's Gospel* [Minneapolis: Augsburg, 1961], p. 1133).

D. The Redemption of Christ's Crucifiers

1. The Father's forgiveness

While being crucified, Jesus Christ redeemed His crucifiers. That speaks volumes about His grace, mercy, and love. When Jesus said, "Father, forgive them; for they know not what they do" (Luke 23:34), what did the Father do? He forgave them. Jesus' prayer was answered in the moment of His death. In the soldiers' fear I see a recognition of sin, and in their confession I see salvation. When someone says, "I'm too evil; the Lord will never forgive me," he needs to understand that Christ forgives the worst of sinners.

2. The Scripture's fulfillment

Christ said, "If I be lifted up from the earth, [I] will draw all men to Myself" (John 12:32, NASB). As He was lifted up on the cross, He drew a thief and a group of soldiers to Himself. It is unspeakable love and grace that won those who killed Jesus on the cross.

The best response anyone can have toward the gospel is saving faith. The centurion set the standard.

II. SHALLOW CONVICTION

A. The Scene

Matthew doesn't comment on this response, but Luke does. Luke 23:47-48 says, "When the centurion saw what was done, he glorified God, saying, Certainly this was a righteous man. And all the people that came together to that sight, beholding the things which were done." All those present at the crucifixion witnessed the darkness, the earthquake, and the opening of the graves. They knew those things couldn't be explained humanly. Something was wrong, and they were the cause. Perhaps they remembered that Jesus raised Lazarus from the dead and virtually banished disease from Palestine during His ministry. Maybe they remembered His cleansing of the Temple and His profound teaching. After all, they once hailed Him as Messiah.

1. Initial conviction

Based on their understanding of the Old Testament, the people should have realized that God was judging them. They should have experienced guilt for their sin, and some did, because Luke 23:48 says, "Beholding the things which were done, [they] smote their breasts, and returned." Their terror mixed with guilt and remorse.

Today people look at the cross and understand Jesus was there because of their sins. They feel bad about that. The cross can be overwhelmingly penetrating, even to an unbelieving heart. Imagine yourself at the scene of the crucifixion screaming for His blood. Then imagine witnessing supernatural phenomena around you. You might realize then that you had violated the holy God. Fear would overpower every other thought in your mind.

2. Eventual rejection

What is so shocking about verse 48 is not that they smote their chests but that they returned. They went home. There was no salvation for them, just conviction. Many who hear the gospel today are convicted and perhaps shed tears. They become anxious, their hearts beat faster, and beads of sweat break out on their brows. They know they're sinners, yet they reject Christ and continue on the path to hell. They go home, turn on the television, eat a sandwich, and watch a football game. The conviction passes, and their life is back to normal. That's essentially what the crowd at the cross did. They felt sorry. They even felt guilty. They knew God was expressing His wrath and that they were the object of it. But that conviction soon passed. After all, at three o'clock the light came back, and there weren't any aftershocks.

B. The Sequel

A few weeks later on the Day of Pentecost, a crowd gathered to hear the apostle Peter. No doubt many of them had been at the foot of the cross and beat on their breasts.

1. Confrontation

As Peter preached, he indicted them for killing Christ. He talked about the resurrection—how God raised Christ from the dead. In Acts 2:36 he sums up his sermon, saying, "God hath made that same Jesus, whom ye have crucified, both Lord and Christ." He confronted them with having crucified their Messiah.

2. Conviction

Verse 37 says, "When they heard this, they were pricked in their heart, and said unto Peter and to the rest of the apostles, Men and brethren, what shall we do?" Being pricked in the heart is like beating on one's chest. They were stabbed with conviction, as if a great blade went right into their hearts. They hurt deeply because they recognized that they had killed their Messiah.

3. Repentance

Peter said to them, "Repent, and be baptized, every one of you, in the name of Jesus Christ for the remission of sins, and ye shall receive the gift of the Holy Spirit" (v. 38). Peter continued to "testify and exhort, saying, Save yourselves from this crooked generation. Then they that gladly received his word were baptized; and the same day there were added unto them about three thousand souls" (vv. 40-41). Some of those who beat their chests at the scene of the cross were in that group. I thank God that some of them were confronted again and felt conviction. This time it led them to salvation.

Some of the people at the foot of the cross never were saved. Once they went home the conviction passed. So many people are like that today. I pray to God that someday a believer will cross their path and preach a message they won't let pass.

Godly Sorrow Versus Worldly Sorrow

The apostle Paul wrote 1 Corinthians to confront the Corinthians about their sin. Word came back to Paul that they were sorry. They had a right response to his letter—they wanted to clean up their church and their lives. Paul wrote this in his second epistle: "For though I made you sorry with a letter, I do not repent. . . . I rejoice, not that ye were made sorry but that ye sorrowed to repentance; for ye were made sorry after a godly manner. . . . For godly sorrow worketh repentance to salvation not to be repented of; but the sorrow of the world worketh death" (2 Cor. 7:8-10).

People who are sorrowful all the time will eventually find that it kills them. Maybe they'll take their own life, die from some illness, or become an alcoholic or drug addict. The sorrow of the world is despair without relief, which leads nowhere except to death. Godly sorrow leads to repentance, which leads to salvation and life.

113

That's the difference between the soldiers and the crowd. The soldiers were repentant. Through the power of the Spirit of God and in answer to the prayer of Jesus, they were saved. The crowd was sorry, but theirs was an ungodly sorrow leading to despair and not salvation.

Ungodly sorrow has no repentance, only resentment. It resents being caught. It is sorry for itself, not for God. Godly sorrow hates the sin more than it hates being caught. You will find godly sorrow exhibited by someone who hates his sin because it is a defiance of holy God, not because it's created some problems in his life. Godly sorrow leads to repentance, which in turn leads to salvation.

III. SYMPATHETIC LOYALTY

Matthew 27:55 says, "Many women were there." The women present at the cross of Christ were characterized by sympathetic loyalty.

A. The Importance of the Women

The women stood afar off at the beginning of the crucifixion (v. 55). The soldiers kept some area clear between the cross and the crowd. The soldiers were closest, the rabble crowd of Jews that passed by were next, and the women were somewhere beyond them. Later, according to John 19:26, they had come close enough to the cross so that Jesus could speak to them. It was at that time He commissioned both Mary and John to care for each other. That tells me the women became more courageous as time went on.

1. Their love

These women were loving and sympathetic, although their hopes and dreams were crushed. They couldn't see beyond tomorrow; they could only watch their Master die. Their loyalties ran so deep and their hearts were so filled with love and sympathy that they stayed with Jesus to the end. They didn't fear the Jews or the Romans. Nothing could overpower their love and sympathy for Christ.

A Characteristic of a Godly Woman

I believe that sympathetic loyalty is one of the most beautiful characteristics of godly women. Show me a godly woman, and I'll show you a life marked by sympathy and loyalty. The women who watched Christ crucified were fearless. They didn't mind being identified with the crucified Christ, who had been mocked, scorned, and ridiculed by their society.

Where were the disciples? According to John 19:26-27, only John was at the cross. The other ten were nowhere to be found. At times John seemed to have the sympathetic heart that is most often found in a woman, yet he was anything but feminine since his nickname was Son of Thunder.

Mark links the centurion with the women. Having talked about the centurion, he says, "There were also women" (Mark 15:40). Certainly he fit better with the women than with the unbelieving crowd.

Commentator G. Campbell Morgan writes this of the women: "Hopeless, disappointed, bereaved, heartbroken; but the love He had created in those hearts for Himself could not be quenched, even by His dying; could not be overcome, even though they were disappointed; could not be extinguished, even though the light of hope had gone out; and over the sea of their sorrow there was no sighing wind that told of the dawn" (*The Gospel According to Matthew* [Old Tappan, N.J.: Revell, 1929], p. 318).

2. Their number

We don't know how women were at the cross. Jesus' ministry included many women. Luke 8:1-3 says that Jesus "went throughout every city and village, preaching and showing the glad tidings of the kingdom of God; and the twelve were with him, and certain women, who had been healed of evil spirits and infirmities: Mary, called Magdalene, out of whom went seven demons;

and Joanna, the wife of Chuza, Herod's steward; and Susanna; and many others, who ministered unto him of their substance." They provided meals, clothing, and money to the Savior and His disciples as they went about their Galilean ministry.

3. Their service

Matthew 27:55 says they followed Jesus from Galilee. When Jesus left Galilee, He came to Jerusalem for Passover. The women, along with their families, followed Jesus south through Peraea, across the Jordan into Jericho, up to Bethany, and then into Jerusalem. Their service began in Galilee and ended up at the foot of the cross. They remained loyal, sympathetic, unwavering, and faithful. David Thomas said, "He was the magnet of their souls. He held them there as the sun holds the planets" (*The Gospel of St. Matthew: A Homiletical Commentary* [Grand Rapids: Kregel, 1979], p. 545).

Matthew 27:55 says they "ministered (Gk., *diakoneō*, "deacon") to him." That word actually refers to waiting on tables (cf. Luke 4:39; 10:40). Serving was the core of their service, not the perimeter. The apostle Paul said the widow who is to be cared for by the church should be "well reported of for good works, if she hath brought up children, if she hath lodged strangers, if she hath washed the saints' feet, if she hath relieved the afflicted, if she hath diligently followed every good work" (1 Tim. 5:10). At the heart of the woman's role is caring for the physical needs of her household as well as being involved in spiritual ministry. Women aren't limited to that, but that is the heart of their service.

4. Their privilege

Many think their role was demeaning, but that wasn't the case at all. Those women were eyewitnesses to the death of Christ. One of them saw the risen Christ before any man did. In the early days of the church the primary sources for news of the death and resurrection of Jesus Christ were those loyal, sympathetic women. You can be sure they held a special place of recognition in the early church. The disciples hid, but the women stood by Christ. Don't underestimate the role of these women. The Lord gave them the privilege of being the original eyewitnesses to the death and resurrection because they proved to be faithful.

B. The Identification of the Women

The Holy Spirit allows us the privilege of meeting a few of the women.

1. Mary Magdalene

This Mary was first mentioned in Luke 8:2. Jesus had cast seven demons out of her and then redeemed her. (Don't confuse her with Mary, the former prostitute, in Luke 7:37). She's always called Mary of Magdala or Mary Magdalene. She was from Magdala, a little town on the western shore of the Sea of Galilee, south of Capernaum. She was called Mary of Magdalene because she had no husband or children. If she had a husband or children, she would have been Mary the wife of so-and-so or Mary the mother of so-and-so. Notice that the second woman mentioned in Matthew 27:56 is Mary the mother of Zebedee's children—another way of saying she is Zebedee's wife.

Notice that one woman is noted for her husband, another by her children, and the other by her town because she had no husband or children. I believe the Lord supports all those roles for women. A woman can have dignity as a single woman. We see that God had a marvelous and unique role for a single woman to play in the plan of God. Mary Magdalene was the first to see the risen Christ. There is also great commendation for a woman who was a mother and a woman who was a wife. Mary Magdalene is an illustration of the importance of single women. Most women, however, are called to be married and have children, unless they are specially gifted in singleness.

2. Mary, the mother of James and Joses

Mark 15:40 calls the third Mary the mother of James the less, so as not to confuse him with James, the brother of

117

John, one of the sons of Zebedee. In John 19:25 she is called the wife of Clopas. James the less is also called James the son of Alphaeus. So Clopas and Alphaeus may be variations on the same name.

3. The mother of Zebedee's children

Mark tells us her name was Salome (Mark 15:40), and John tells us she was the sister of Mary the mother of Jesus (John 19:25). That means James and John were Jesus' cousins.

The women in Mark 15:40 are identified by marriage or by children because that is the distinct and wonderful role of most women. These women provided out of their substance for those who labored for the cause of Christ. God highly honored them by allowing them to be special witnesses of His death and resurrection.

Extolling the Virtue of Women

When God wanted to extol the highest virtue of women, He said the following in Psalm 113:1-5, 9: "Praise ye the Lord. Praise, O ye the servants of the Lord, praise the name of the Lord. Blessed be the name of the Lord from this time forth and for evermore. From the rising of the sun unto the going down of the same, the Lord's name is to praised. The Lord is high above all nations, and his glory above the heavens. Who is like unto the Lord, our God, who dwelleth on high? . . . He maketh the barren woman to keep house, and to be a joyful mother of children. Praise ye the Lord." God made the barren woman a keeper of the house and a bearer of children. This is not to disparage those whom God has not blessed with children, or those who are single; it's just that Scripture says childbearing is God's highest calling for women. That's supported in the way they're identified in the narrative of the gospel record.

God allowed the women to be eyewitnesses of His Son's death and resurrection because they were faithful. What about you? When the world is hostile toward Christ, do you fade away or do you remain steadfast? Can the world see you belong to Jesus Christ? Is your love and loyalty for Christ so strong that you stay attached to Him no matter what the cost? Are you unwavering in your commitment?

IV. SELFISH FEAR

You won't find this response in any verse, but it can be deduced by the absence of the disciples. Nothing is said about them because they weren't at the cross. Where were they?

A. Denying the Power of Faith

I would have thought Peter would be there. Matthew 26:75 says that after he denied Christ three times and heard the cock crow, "he went out, and wept bitterly." He poured out his heart to God for forgiveness. You would think that once he had gone through that he would stand by Christ. But after weeping he went back into hiding.

Matthew 26:56 tells us what happened to the disciples: "All the disciples forsook Him and fled." They were cowards when they should have been courageous. Jesus foretold Peter's denial by saying, "Satan hath desired to have you, that he may sift you as wheat" (Luke 22:31). You separate wheat from chaff by shaking it. Satan was going to shake Peter in every way he could. But in verse 32 Christ says, "I have prayed for thee, that thy faith fail not." Did the disciples lose their salvation? No, because the Lord upheld them.

B. Violating the Principle of Discipleship

The disciples entered into a terrible time of cowardice. They were in a spiritual struggle. They violated the basic principle of discipleship from Matthew 10:38: "He that taketh not his cross and followeth after me, is not worthy of me." If anyone is going to be His disciple, he must be willing to give his life if necessary. At that time, the disciples weren't. When they thought they might lose their lives, they fled. Satan was shaking them violently. But Jesus prayed that their faith wouldn't fail. No matter how violently Satan may shake the believer in times of doubt and fear, he will never lose his faith because it's in the hands of Jesus Christ.

119

It is sad that the disciples didn't stand by Jesus at His death. He died with only the women and John present. After all He had done for them, it's a tragedy that they weren't there.

There are times when we should stand for Christ in a particular situation, but we don't. Instead we hide. The sifting keeps us from enduring. We want to save reputation, name, or career. We don't want to be named with Jesus Christ.

Ask yourself where you are. Do you need to respond to Christ with saving faith? Do you want to say with centurion, "Truly, this was the Son of God"? Are you like the crowd? Are you going to let the conviction pass? If you're a believer, are you like the women? Do you loyally stand by Christ, whatever the cost? Or are you like the disciples, hiding somewhere so that no one can find out whom you belong to?

"O Sacred Head, Now Wounded" is one of the most beautiful and moving hymns about the cross that's ever been penned. It is attributed to Bernard of Clairvaux and was translated into English by James Alexander in the nineteenth century.

> O sacred Head, now wounded,
> With grief and shame weighed down,
> Now scornfully surrounded
> With thorns thine only crown,
> O sacred Head, what glory,
> What bliss till now was thine!
> Yet, though despised and gory,
> I joy to call thee mine.
>
> What Thou, my Lord, hast suffered
> Was all for sinners' gain:
> Mine, mine was the transgression,
> But Thine the deadly pain.
> Lo, here I fall, my Savior!
> 'Tis I deserve Thy place;
> Look on me with Thy favor,
> Vouchsafe to me Thy grace.
>
> What language shall I borrow
> To thank Thee, dearest Friend,
> For this Thy dying sorrow,
> Thy pity without end?

O make me Thine forever;
And should I fainting be,
Lord, let me never, never
Outlive my love to Thee.

Focusing on the Facts

1. What is the best response any unbeliever can make to the crucifixion of Christ (see p. 104)?
2. What happened that changed many of the soldiers' perspective of Jesus (Matt. 27:54; see p. 106)?
3. Describe the fear that the soldiers experienced (see pp. 106-7).
4. What did their fear indicate (see p. 107)?
5. What did their fear lead them to (see pp. 107-8)?
6. What was the centurion affirming when he said, "Truly, this was the Son of God" (Matt. 27:54; see p. 107)?
7. What is the only way anyone can know that Jesus is God's Son (Matt. 16:16-17; see p. 108)?
8. Explain how some discredit the centurion's statement that Jesus was the Son of God (see pp. 109-10).
9. Whom did Jesus Christ redeem while on the cross (see p. 110)?
10. Why should the people at the foot of the cross have realized that God was judging them (see p. 111)?
11. How did the people respond to the phenomena that occurred at the crucifixion (Luke 23:48; see p. 111)?
12. How do we know that the conviction some people experienced at the cross didn't lead to salvation (Luke 23:48; see p. 112)?
13. When Peter preached on the Day of Pentecost (Acts 2:36), what did he indict the people for (see p. 112)?
14. What did the crowd do after they were convicted by Peter's sermon (Acts 2:41; see p. 113)?
15. What are the main differences between godly sorrow and worldly sorrow (2 Cor. 7:8-10; see pp. 113-14)?
16. What is an important characteristic of a godly woman (see p. 115)?
17. How did the women serve Jesus during His ministry (see p. 116)?
18. What great privilege did Christ grant to the women who remained loyal to Him while He hung on the cross (see pp. 116-17)?

19. Who was Mary Magdalene? Why is it significant that she is described by the town she was from (Luke 8:2; see p. 117)?
20. According to Psalm 113:9, how does God extol the virtue of women (see p. 118)?
21. Why weren't the disciples present at the cross of Christ (see p. 119)?
22. What basic principle of discipleship did the disciples violate (Matt. 10:38; see p. 119)?

Pondering the Principles

1. Perhaps the most famous words Christ uttered are, "Father, forgive them; for they know not what they do" (Luke 23:34). God answered Jesus' prayer, and He answered it not only for some Roman soldiers but also for you. The treatment Christ suffered at the hands of those who crucified Him is no worse than the treatment He has received from every sinner. Meditate on the crucifixion scene. Remember what your sin cost Christ. Then remember that in spite of yourself, God saved you through the death of Christ on the cross. Thank God for His grace and forgiveness. And thank Christ for taking your place on that cross.

2. Reread 2 Corinthians 7:8-10 and the section dealing with godly and worldly sorrow (see pp. 113-14). When you are convicted of sin, how do you respond? Do you exhibit godly sorrow or worldly sorrow? What grieves you most: the fact that you disobeyed God or the inconvenience that your sin caused you? Seek to respond in all circumstances in a way that is pleasing to God, and that includes your sorrow.

3. The followers of Christ responded in two ways when He was taken captive and crucified. A few women along with John remained loyal and stayed with Him until His death. The rest fled in fear. Where are you when you need to be counted as one who belongs to Christ? Do you stand by the cross, or do you hide from the world? Matthew 10:38 gives us a principle of discipleship that all believers should follow. Memorize it.

Scripture Index